I0042820

OF BANKS
AND CRISES

OF BANKS AND CRISES

Cristina Peicuti
ESCP Business School, France

Jacques Beyssade

World Scientific

NEW JERSEY · LONDON · SINGAPORE · BEIJING · SHANGHAI · HONG KONG · TAIPEI · CHENNAI · TOKYO

Published by

World Scientific Publishing Europe Ltd.
57 Shelton Street, Covent Garden, London WC2H 9HE
Head office: 5 Toh Tuck Link, Singapore 596224
USA office: 27 Warren Street, Suite 401-402, Hackensack, NJ 07601

Library of Congress Control Number: 2024003533

British Library Cataloguing-in-Publication Data
A catalogue record for this book is available from the British Library.

Cover image: *The Fight over Money*, © Museum Plantin-Moretus, Antwerp, Belgium.

OF BANKS AND CRISES

Copyright © 2024 by Cristina Peicuti & Jacques Beyssade

ISBN 978-1-80061-561-8 (hardcover)
ISBN 978-1-80061-574-8 (paperback)
ISBN 978-1-80061-562-5 (ebook for institutions)
ISBN 978-1-80061-563-2 (ebook for individuals)

For any available supplementary material, please visit
https://www.worldscientific.com/worldscibooks/10.1142/Q0461#t=suppl

Desk Editors: Nambirajan Karuppiah/Shi Ying Koe

Typeset by Stallion Press
Email: enquiries@stallionpress.com

About the Authors

Cristina Peicuti foresaw the 2008 crisis, which was the subject of her thesis, "The Subprime Mortgage Crisis and the Credit Channel" (Paris, Panthéon-Assas University, 2006–2009). Affiliate Professor and Scientific Director at the ESCP Business School, founded in Paris in 1819, she is a senior economist at one of the world's thirty globally systemic banks (G-SIBs). She is also a foreign trade adviser to the French government and a member of Société d'Économie Politique, founded in Paris in 1842, an organisation concerned with political economy. Cristina is the author of several books: *The European Economy in 100 Quotations* (2024), *Decoding Economic Crises* (2023) and *Credit, Destabilisation and Crises* (2010).

Jacques Beyssade has been the Secretary General of one of the world's thirty globally systemic banks (G-SIBs) since 2018. In a group with 100,000 employees and 35 million customers, he is in charge of Legal and Public Affairs, Corporate Governance, Compliance, Security and Permanent Control. He draws on his extensive experience of banking through boom and bust cycles stretching back 30 years and across three continents. A recognised banking expert, he has been a foreign trade adviser to the French government for the last two decades.

"It is a familiar remark that only "the rich can borrow," and the experience of every day seems to prove it. Yet the poor also may have need of credit, even more than the rich. How, then, can they obtain it?

This problem is easily solved by cooperation. An isolated laborer or artisan, no matter how honest or industrious he may be, cannot furnish sufficient guarantee for a loan. Sickness, loss of work, and death, may at any time overtake him and make it impossible, despite his best intentions, to pay back what he has borrowed. But if laborers or artisans to the number of ten, a hundred, or a thousand, are grouped in an organization, and held together, if need be, by the ties of collective responsibility, the security they have to offer will be considerably greater, and they will find it much easier to obtain credit without falling into the hands of usurers. The dues which are paid to such an organization, moreover, will ultimately build up to a large amount of capital which the organization can lend to its members."[1]

Charles Gide [1847–1932], *Principes d'économie politique* published 1894. The French economist was a professor of political economy at the Collège de France and was the historic leader of the French cooperative bank movement, considered one of the five founders of Banques Populaires.

---

[1]Gide, Charles (1984) *Principles of Economic Policy*. Boston USA: D.C. Heath & Co, publishers, translated by C. Williams A. Verditz.

Translated by Malcolm Leveridge with the support of the chair of BPCE Group at the ESCP Business School on Mutual and Cooperative Banking for the Benefit of the Economy

GROUPE
BPCE

ESCP
BUSINESS SCHOOL

Foreword

Poor bankers! Poor economists! You won't see people at their windows and on their balconies clapping for members of these two professions.[2] Economists are decried for never having anticipated crises. Blame is levelled at bankers, perceived as blind to the obvious and driven by greed. Given the constant trial by media to which the two professions are subjected, Cristina Peicuti and Jacques Beyssade's book gives the floor to the defence. It is not because the authors are beholden to corporate interests, but because they are motivated by their desire to understand and take action. The relevance of these criticisms, occasional or recurrent, is not being challenged. The authors' purpose is to analyse the behaviours and mistakes that may have given rise to these reproofs and identify changes that would enable both professions to contribute more effectively and in a timely manner to the common good.

For that matter, the three crises compared by the authors — the Great Depression of 1929, the Great Recession of 2008 and the COVID-19 crisis of 2020 and its fallout in coming years — are, from this standpoint, very different. The banks (and therefore also the economists in their employ or advising them) were largely responsible for the first two, but not in the least for the third, which on the contrary they are helping to limit and may help exit in less of a bad shape than might be feared! This amounts to a mirror image, providing a degree of symmetry. The 1929 and 2008 crises were first and foremost economic crises, with obvious

---

[2]During the pandemic, in what became a daily ritual, the French population took to their balconies and windows at 8 pm to applaud doctors and nurses fighting the outbreak.

consequences for the health of the population (poverty obviously leads to poor health). The current crisis is first of all a health crisis, with very damaging economic consequences. Is it because a pandemic is never good for the economy? True, but not only.

Let's try to take a step back. It would not be true to contend that the current pandemic is of an unprecedented severity. Cast your mind back to the 14th century when the Black Death decimated half of Europe's population in a matter of years. More recently, the Spanish flu in 1918–1919 killed more than 40 million people worldwide (compared with just over 3 million for COVID-19 at the time of writing). As for the Asian flu in 1957 and the Hong Kong flu in 1968, which are largely forgotten today, it is estimated that each caused between 1 and 4 million deaths, at a time when the world's population was considerably smaller (3 billion in 1960, almost 8 billion today) and much younger, at least in Europe, than at present.

The fact remains, as pointed out quite rightly by the book's two authors, that COVID-19 will undoubtedly be "the most serious pandemic of the last century". That it should have significant economic consequences, well that was to be expected. What is astonishing is their sheer scale: that a mere virus, admittedly contagious, but of limited severity (case fatality rate of around 0.5%) and affecting mainly the elderly (in contrast to the Spanish flu, which killed mainly young adults, the average age of COVID-related deaths is just over 81, so very close to the general mortality rate) should have brought the whole world to a virtual standstill for several months! What is unprecedented is not the severity of the pandemic, but the scale of the ensuing economic crisis.

To the best of my knowledge, it is the first time such a severe economic crisis can be traced back mainly to a health emergency, to the political response (the economic crisis having been precipitated not so much by the pandemic as by measures to check its transmission: lockdowns, furloughs, closure of schools, retail outlets, borders, etc.) and it might be argued to a media-induced iatrogenesis (politicians, especially in France, initially heeded the injunctions of a section of the medical profession, which were relayed ad nauseam by the media)! This is what's new and what we need to try and understand.

When the first lockdown took place, a number of intellectuals, some of whom are amongst my dearest friends, rejoiced, for this was the first time, they said, that health was given priority over the economy. They were right in their assessment, but their jubilation was misplaced.

When the economy is sacrificed, it follows that the poor are thrown to the wolves (as recalled by the authors, in any crisis it is the poorest who pay the heaviest price) along with women (they too paid a particularly heavy price during the pandemic) and the young (their studies, from the primary to the university, and life, private as well as professional, were seriously disrupted, if not upended), to the benefit mainly, it should be stressed, of their parents and grandparents (93% of COVID-related deaths concerned people 65 and over). The father that I am, and old enough to be a grandfather, can hardly take any comfort in all this! Nor can the citizen that I am! One million new poor in France, while it is estimated that the crisis pushed an additional 150 million people in the world into extreme poverty. This surely is no victory of humanism.

Should we have carried on as if nothing had happened, allowing the virus to spread freely in the expectation of a probable, but belated, collective immunity? Obviously not, for that would have been morally shocking and politically inconceivable. The authors point out that countries led by populists whose response to the pandemic was a form of denial (Trump in the United States and Bolsonaro in Brazil, to name but two) were often the ones with the highest number of COVID-related deaths, and even so experienced recessions. On the other hand, there is cause for satisfaction in that, having sheltered excessively behind "scientists", as they called them, political leaders did gradually win back some autonomy. After what seemed an eternity, they finally became as concerned about the economy as health, about the young nearly as much as the old (easing lockdowns and lifting them earlier than most epidemiologists would have wanted), and about the vaccination campaign far more than isolation, while succeeding thus far in avoiding what was feared above all, being that emergency and reanimation services would be overwhelmed.

The disproportion between the cause (a health emergency) and the effects (economic, therefore also social and societal, not to mention a restriction of civil liberties that was unprecedented in times of peace) of this crisis remains no less striking. Why so? The authors explain that, in most countries, health became an "absolute priority", even a supreme value, what I call "panmedicalism". I won't elaborate, other than to say that this confuses possessions (such as wealth, health) and values (such as love, justice) to the benefit of the former (health in the present case). Subjugating values to possessions or elevating possessions to the rank of values (a fortiori of supreme values) is a form of nihilism: financial nihilism, if we say money reigns supreme, which almost everyone condemns;

health nihilism, if health is put above everything else, which almost everyone seems to approve of. This is a particularity of our times, which has been cause for much rejoicing in recent months, yet which I find troubling. If health is the supreme value, sacrificing liberty and justice on this altar out of necessity would be normal. But, would it be just? Would it be consistent with our democratic ideals? That might just about be conceivable when there is a public health emergency (for which reason I never spoke out against the successive lockdowns). However, there is an element of danger, in my view, were this to become the general rule. Even assuming the public health system could be run more efficiently under a dictatorship than a democracy, would this be reason enough to forsake a democratic system or to stop combating this form of oppression!

Why has health been elevated to an "absolute priority"? It is probably because of religion's decline: the less you believe in an afterlife, the more you cling onto mortal life; the less you believe in salvation, the more you put store in health. Then, probably because of the ageing of the population: being, very often, the ones who fall ill, the elderly naturally worry about their health. Also, because of the formidable progress of medicine, a science which is listened to more attentively as it becomes more efficient. Finally, fear of death, of disease, is ever present, but as rightly pointed out by the authors is of poor counsel.

As to the historical background, and with stronger reason for lack of competence, the solutions proposed by the authors and the obstacles (notably regulatory) they denounce, it would not be my place to venture an opinion. Let's just say that I found the book very interesting, stimulating and even, given the prevailing doom and gloom, comforting reading. The fact that banks can and must play a major role in the crisis exit will only shock a handful of activists trapped in an outdated ideology. Besides, many of our biggest banks today are mutual or cooperative undertakings, rather than being private or capitalistic (owned by their customers rather than shareholders). And, all of them contribute, positively or negatively, to the life of our society. What kind of economy can there be without exchanges? What exchanges, once we move away from barter, can there be without money? What kind of money — when it has to be a store of value — can there be without banks?

One might add, what kind of banking would there be without risks? Cristina Peicuti and Jacques Beyssade have no qualms: "banking is by definition a risky business. Liquidity and credit risks reflect the imbalance that exists, in any society, between savers who wish to retain rapid, risk-free access to their deposits, and borrowers wanting to finance projects, generally over a longer time horizon, that sometimes fail. Therein lays the usefulness of bankers, the justification for their remuneration, and the explanation for the boom in banking during all periods of strong growth when projects are nineteen to the dozen."

Can risk be removed? Probably not, nor should it. Risk mitigation, to the extent possible, is another matter, but importantly one must not be misled as to what the main dangers are. This book highlights a number of them, some of which have been exacerbated by the crisis and all of which will outlive it: "exacerbated nationalism, deepening inequalities, a frenzy of redundant projects," not forgetting what is undoubtedly the most worrying of all: the environmental crisis and resulting climate disruption.

This has not prevented the authors from seeking what they call, in the manner of the Ancients, "healthy growth in a healthy world," or even mapping out "a happy, healthy and sustainable growth path." I have no doubt that bankers and economists can contribute to this. But, let's not forget that this is a matter for all of us, and that it is therefore political at least as much as it is economic or financial. "For several thousand years, no civilisation has developed without being able to rely on a powerful banking system," our two experts note. But, neither, I would add, without political institutions, albeit of varying and therefore unequal constitutional design. Banks are a necessary means, like states, like democracy itself. Freedom is not a means, but an end.

André Comte-Sponville
Philosopher, and author of the worldwide bestseller *A Small Treatise on Great Virtues: The Uses of Philosophy in Everyday Life*

Contents

About the Authors   v

Foreword   xi

Introduction: Crisis Raising Many Questions   xix

Part I   What Crisis?   **1**
危机

Chapter 1   1929, 2008 and 2019: Damning Repetitions   3

Chapter 2   Great Depression, Great Recession: Banks Guilty
of Triggering the Crisis   9
Guilty of the Great Depression   10
Guilty of the Great Recession   11

Chapter 3   COVID-19 Crisis: Banks Have the Capacity to
Finance Recovery   15
Health emergency or crisis of the healthcare system?   15
Economic crisis or crisis of an economic system?   22

Chapter 4   Banks: The Cornerstone of the Recovery?   27

Part II   In the Cold Light of Day   **31**
Νεμεσις

Chapter 5   France: Centuries of History … and of Debt   33

Chapter 6   Out of the Great Depression into a World War   39

Chapter 7   After the Great Recession, a Global Revolt Against
the Established Order   43

France and the disenchantment of the French electorate   43
The United States that voted Trump   48
The United Kingdom that voted for Brexit   53

Chapter 8   Will There Be a Global Change Post-COVID?   57

Part III   Banks: Mirror of Our Society?   **65**
In God We Trust

Chapter 9   The Profession's Metamorphosis   67

The oldest profession in the world   67
Banking: New lease of life in the past decade   70

Chapter 10 Cooperative Banking: A Profession Reinvented by
and for Its Customers   75

Chapter 11 The Illusion of Control   83

Are banks responsible?   83
Have banks had their wings clipped?   86
Are banks dangerous?   90

Part IV   Seven Proposals for a Healthy Recovery   **93**
Crescentia sana in mundo sano

Chapter 12 Rethinking Public Health Policy   95

Chapter 13 Repositioning Europe Centre Stage in the World   103

Chapter 14 Loosening the Regulatory Brakes   109

Chapter 15 Smarter Regulations   115

Chapter 16 Financing the New Environmental Cycle   119

Chapter 17 Financing Building Renovation   123

Chapter 18 Beyond Our Borders   127

Conclusion   133
Bibliography   141
Name Index   147

Introduction: Crisis Raising Many Questions

After the first lockdown in 2020, French writer Michel Houellebecq published an open letter, sharing his vision of writing in the times of COVID-19. Asked "Will interesting books see the light of day, inspired by this period?" he answers "I wonder too. I really wondered, but deep down I don't think so. On the plague we've had a lot of things, over the centuries, the plague has interested writers a lot. Now I have my doubts."[1] Too early to say, but it has to be conceded that, as regards his analysis of society, Michel Houellebecq has often been eerily prophetic. For example, in his novel *Sérotonine*, published in 2019, the author masterfully describes the causes and consequences of the disillusionment of the generation behind the Yellow Vest movement in France. Yet, few people saw this movement coming.

Michel Houellebecq does not believe that we will wake up, after COVID-19, to a new world, "it will be the same, only a little worse."[2]

It would not be our place to contradict Michel Houellebecq, but we would like to shed some light on the COVID-19 crisis by explaining its analogies with the Great Depression and Great Recession, and the banks' role in reviving the economy post-COVID.

---

[1] www.francetvinfo.fr/sante/maladie/coronavirus/coronavirus-pourmichel-houellebecq-le-monde-d-apres-sera-le-meme-en-un-peupire_3948117.html.
[2] *Ibid.*

The current crisis is thought-provoking. For a banker and an economist, it could not be otherwise, just as it is for members of the medical profession, employers and employees, political and religious leaders, artists and writers.

Plenty to mull over for the economist, for the response to the crisis has been most unusual: economic and financial dogmas have been thrown out the window even by the most orthodox governments. In most countries, the health of citizens, young or old, in fine fettle or fragile, was elevated to an absolute priority. In France, it was a case of "whatever the cost", a policy that clearly made an impression. This was in fact the approach of most governments in developed countries. There were some exceptions, often in countries with atypical leaders. In the United States, the Trump administration started by denying there even was a health emergency, stubbornly limiting to the extent possible any restrictions on individual liberties in the name of economic normalcy. At the same time, the administration did much to stimulate research, helping to develop vaccines in record times, so that the United States was the first country to embark on massive vaccination campaigns. In Sweden, as it sought to achieve herd immunity, economic activity was spared to begin with, the gamble being that transmission would cease of itself once a necessarily high proportion of the population had been infected. History will tell, once the virus and successive variants have been and gone, whether these atypical policies were more effective or less so than those protecting each and everyone's health "whatever the cost". Effectiveness for the economist refers to the equilibrium between the resources deployed, the long-term consequences and, of course, the death toll.

During this crisis, every government had to make choices. Abide by the laws of nature, allow the epidemic to follow its course and ultimately peter out, accepting there would be a significant human cost, or check its progress? Defend individual liberties, in the knowledge that the defence of these principles would necessarily lead to gatherings and increase transmission, or impose drastic curbs of liberties? Respect the rules of sound economic management, which consist in not getting into debt beyond one's means, or ignore these rules? Though these three principles, whether natural or philosophical, had never been questioned, the governments of most countries, including France, chose to oppose them with all their might. To varying degrees, entire economies were placed under drip-feed, the cost of which will have to be paid by future generations. Now to the economist, the question is how, having recovered, can one then survive, saddled with a debt that has exploded?

As with economists, it was the bankers' convictions that were shaken. There is always a lot of finger-pointing anyway, yet in this crisis not the slightest blame attaches to bankers. Their treatment by the authorities in many countries left them not a moment of respite. Much as doctors and nurses were requisitioned to care for the most severe cases in the emergency wards, bankers burned the midnight oil during the first months of the crisis to keep afloat France's many small and medium-sized enterprises, only to see the very principles of the country's economy trampled underfoot by the authorities. Overnight, in total disregard of their professional judgement, bankers were directed to lend without discernment, under the protection of a state guarantee covering in the main any risks. Much as doctors attend all their patients in the same way, not distinguishing between the most robust and those who are already at death's door, bankers were expected to provide loans to those having fallen temporarily on hard times as well as those who would never be able to repay the loan. Bankers toiled night and day, as did doctors, without much triaging. All this went on when alternating phases of lockdowns and curfews brought about radical changes to which bankers had to adapt, lest they be overtaken by their rivals, for competition was no less fierce. There were changes at the technological level, with the advent in the public domain of strong authentication and contactless payment, the boom in e-commerce and the sudden introduction of remote working as an absolute necessity rather than a likeable utopia. Gender inequalities were exacerbated, for more women had to take furlough to look after their children when schools were closed, and more women were employed in the healthcare sector, required to work longer hours and more exposed to the risk of contamination. Banks also had customers with seasonal activities or deemed non-essential, whose standard of living plummeted suddenly. All these changes required bankers, at least universal bankers serving all social strata, to rethink their offer, tariff scales, sometimes their general philosophy.

The banker's calling being to finance entrepreneurs and large projects, how can he contribute to reviving an economy plunged into a state of lethargy from having been drip-fed? Everyone is urging bankers to step into the breach, yet they have their hands tied behind their back as a result of the regulations introduced in response to the previous crisis.

Questions aplenty for the financiers we are, for while none of us bear any responsibility for the current crisis, none had seen it coming. The Great Depression of 1929 and the Great Recession of 2008 had been preceded by small tremors and some big bubbles, enough for some of us to predict what is modestly called a "severe correction". Cristina Peicuti predicted the 2008 crisis in her thesis "The financial crisis and the credit channel", which she began in 2006 and defended in 2009 at the University of Paris II.[3] There was nothing of the sort here. If pandemics were among the operational risk situations that we imagined facing one day, it was from the point of view of staff safety and business continuity, not from the point of view of resolving the economic impact.

This book seeks to provide answers to all of these questions raised by the COVID-19 crisis. Our answers are based on analysis and backed by figures as economics teaches us to do, but they are also rooted in our knowledge of our customers and our desire to contribute to their development, true to the banking sector's calling.

---

[3] Peicuti, C. (2009). *La crise financière et le canal crédit*, www.theses.fr/2009PA020102.

Part I

What Crisis?

危机*

---

*The Chinese word for "crisis" (pinyin: wēijī) combines two Chinese characters meaning "danger" (wēi, 危) and "opportunity" (jī, 机).

Chapter 1

1929, 2008 and 2019: Damning Repetitions

The history of crises centres around living beyond one's financial, organisational and climatic means. The excesses of recent decades have accelerated their occurrence. These crises trigger human catastrophes, referred to neutrally as "disruptions", synonymous with the poor getting poorer and with the emergence of new poor. The three major global crises that we go on to analyse have spawned inequalities that have been far more entrenched and contagious than the COVID-19 virus. Each has led to a rise in populism in Europe, bringing about the economic, political and cultural decline of the European continent.

Europe has paid a higher price than most for these crises, two of which can be traced back to the United States, one to China. What is striking is that the countries at the origin of these crises have in fact emerged stronger.

The 1929 crisis forever deprived Europe of its position as the world's leading power and dimmed its cultural influence, which until then had been undisputed. The crisis that found its origins in the United States led to such inflation and such poverty in Germany that the far right party led by Adolf Hitler was swept to power through the ballot box. This explains the visceral aversion of Germans to inflation, whereas the French associate inflation with times of prosperity. Louis-Ferdinand Céline published two novels at the time of the Great Depression, *Voyage au bout de la nuit*[1]

---

[1] *Journey to the End of the Night* (1932).

and *Mort à crédit*,[2] depicting the demise of the middle class, condemned to death on credit in the wake of this financial crisis. Will that be the case for the COVID-19 crisis?

Lessons were drawn from the catastrophic handling of the 1929 crisis, so that the short-term management of the 2008 crisis by central banks and governments was better. Longer term, however, inequalities were exacerbated, with populist movements able to capitalise on the resulting distress, being swept back to power in several European Union (EU) member states, or tantalisingly close. One of the consequences was Brexit, besides weakening not just the United Kingdom but also the European Union, was to reinforce the dominance of the United States and China. In the United States, the impoverishment of the country's middle classes in the wake of the 2008 crisis was seized upon by Donald Trump, helping him to the White House. During his term of office, the longstanding alliance between the United States and Europe was put on hold. Globalisation was put to the test, and with it multilateralism. Populism always feeds on a desire to recover the lost "greatness" of a nation in decline.

To the surprise of the United States, the next systemic crisis was not home-grown, but can be traced back to China, a country vying to become the world's leading power since joining the World Trade Organization in 2001. Much as the United States was the first country to emerge from the Great Depression and Great Recession it had triggered, so was China the first to emerge from the crisis triggered by COVID-19, though statistics coming out of this country should not be taken at face value.

If reason prevails, developed countries should press ahead with their initiative to have the vaccine considered a global public good. It is vital to vaccinate as much as possible in poor countries where population density and precarious living conditions have led to an exponential rise in cases. These countries, more than others, are propitious for the development of new variants that can but end up affecting rich countries. This "vaccine diplomacy" is currently dominated by China, which has gradually strengthened its grip over certain emerging countries, by the same significantly reducing the influence of western countries. For China, this is a new chapter or Silk Road in its Belt and Road Initiative.

In the world's leading power, the economic achievements of the Trump administration have been wiped out by the pandemic. The US

---

[2] *Death on Credit* (1936). aka *Death on the Installment Plan* for the American edition.

President tested positive for COVID-19 and recovered, but the virus that came from China sounded his political demise. The Republican leadership did not excel in its management of the health crisis, even though, paradoxically, their rhetoric was all about protecting the middle class. They started by denying there even was a health emergency, only to face up to the reality of the virus when they fell ill themselves.

More generally, countries governed by populist parties are those that recorded the highest death toll. In light of the intense circulation of the virus in the United Kingdom, it is not surprising that this country was the first to see the appearance of a more contagious and lethal variant. In the same way, Jair Bolsonaro's management of the crisis produced the Brazilian variant. It has to be conceded that leaders with populist, manly discourses may have cowed their population, but not the virus.

Besides the rise of populism, the second analogy is that during crises it is the people in the most precarious situations who suffer most. Crises always reveal inequalities, accelerating the trend towards impoverishment of the vulnerable populations and middle class, as shown by the health and economic crises triggered by COVID-19.

As a result, crises usually favour the return in the short term of the Welfare State. Much like individual liberties, economic liberalism was put on hold temporarily, only to start up again with renewed vigour once the health emergency was over. In the midst of the COVID-19 crisis, France's economy minister announced that the pension reform would go ahead after the crisis, as people would have to work longer. In general, the tax burden rises and social transfers are cut post-crisis in an effort to plug the deficit caused by the fiscal expansionism pursued at the height of the health emergency. It is the poorest who then pay the heaviest price though they need longer to extricate themselves from the misery into which they were plunged by the crisis. Even in countries such as France, shortcomings in the social protection system measures mean that the most precarious members of society are still not being helped. Post-COVID, it would therefore be desirable to continue with the "whatever the cost" approach but target the most disadvantaged, who will take far longer to exit the crisis.

Major crises invariably lead to a rise in unemployment. The ensuing recovery first benefits men, then women. The COVID-19 crisis has been particularly severe for women. In many countries, schools were closed for more than one year. Most of the time, it is women who sacrificed their careers to look after their children. When a woman stops working, her career does not pick up from where it left off. The risk is that the COVID-19 crisis will wipe out years of progress in the condition of women in the workplace.

It is also mostly women who have cared for COVID-19 patients. In a study, Women at the core of the fight against COVID-19 crisis,[3] the Organisation for Economic Co-operation and Development (OECD) found that women made up almost 70% of the healthcare workforce (around 85% of nurses and midwives, over 50% of physicians, dentists and pharmacists) in countries for which data was available. They were therefore exposed to a greater risk of infection than men. They also faced increased risks of violence, exploitation, abuse or harassment during lockdowns.

In other professions, the COVID-19 crisis disproportionately affected women's jobs and incomes, when even before a significant pay gap existed between women and men.

According to Phumzile Mlambo-Ngcuka, who served as the Executive Director of UN Women with the rank of Under-Secretary-General of the United Nations, and Gabriela Ramos, the OECD Chief of Staff and Sherpa to the G20: "Many women — 740 million of whom work in the informal economy with jobs that offer little to no social protection — now face severe economic insecurity and few options. In Mexico, for example, 99% of the country's largely female domestic workers are not enrolled in any social security program. Some industries, like garment manufacturing in Bangladesh where women constitute 85% of the workforce, will also be hit hard. The situation is even more distressing for older women, as twice as many women as men 65 and over live alone in G20 countries, often without any adequate pension."[4]

In an analysis published by France Stratégie in November 2018, the point was made that, even before the COVID-19 crisis, "the pay gap between men and women, while hardly perceptible at the start of the career, then widens steadily so that, by the end of the career, women are paid 110% of the average salary, men 130%."[5]

According to the French office for statistics INSEE, the average pay gap between women and men in the public and private sectors had

---

[3] https://www.oecd.org/coronavirus/policy-responses/women-at-the-core-of-the-fight-against-covid-19-crisis-553a8269/.

[4] www.reuters.com/article/us-health-coronavirus-women-breakingview/breakingviews-guest-view-can-we-achieve-gender-equality-idUSKCN21Q3FA.

[5] www.strategie.gouv.fr/publications/discriminations-selon-lage.

narrowed before the COVID-19 crisis. Will the gender pay gap in France widen anew post-crisis? The fact that there is no updated data concerning equal pay for women and men shows that this subject is far from a priority. In 2021, the most recent data available goes back to 2017. INSEE found that "in 2017, women employed in the private sector on average earned 16.8% less than men on a full time equivalent basis, so for the same amount of work […]. In addition to the gap in hourly pay, there are inequalities in working hours, as women are more often employed on a part-time basis and spend less time in employment over the year than men. When these last factors affecting pay are taken into account, women on average earn 28.5% less than men."[6]

The gender pay gap is defined as the difference between median earnings of men and women relative to median earnings of men. According to the OECD, the gender pay gap varies widely across member countries, ranging from 3.5% in Romania to 32.5% in South Korea.

Romania is the country with the smallest gender pay gap of all the countries belonging to the OECD, at 3.5%. It is closely followed by Colombia, Belgium, Costa Rica, Denmark and Norway, all below 5%, then by Hungary, Italy, Greece, New Zealand, Sweden, Croatia and Ireland, all below 10%. What will be observed is that many countries are better pupils when it comes to women's pay than France, though it has enshrined equality and fraternity in its constitution.

In most countries — save three: United Kingdom, Portugal and Switzerland — gender pay gaps are greater in higher-paying jobs than in low-paying jobs, reflecting the so-called glass ceiling. The lesser gender pay gap for low-paying jobs is due in most cases to institutional factors, such as the minimum salary and collective bargaining. Generally speaking, a better redistribution of wealth, to which pay equity would contribute, would be conducive to economic growth in the post-COVID world.

As for businesses, which will drive economic recovery, they took on more debt during the COVID-19 crisis than during the subprime crisis.

The corporate default rate during the COVID-19 crisis may appear less, but that is only because, at the time, this crisis was barely getting under way. The worst is probably yet to come, as the loans and advances that have been granted, often with the help of States, will not come up for repayment for quite some time. Furthermore, the huge support extended

---

[6]https://www.insee.fr/en/statistiques/4806493.

by the public authorities to Eurozone economies means that default rates were lower in Europe than in the United States.

The increases in the monetary base and public debt underscore the unprecedented financial effort deployed to support the European and US economies through the COVID-19 crisis.

Admittedly, the 2008 crisis was more ably managed than its predecessor in 1929, but even so, it exacerbated inequalities, in turn reviving populism, with as figureheads Boris Johnson, Matteo Salvini, Donald Trump, and Jair Bolsonaro, but it did not lead to the third world war... While the 2008 crisis was ably managed in the short term, it had very unfortunate effects over the medium term, which are examined later. It would be preferable not to make the same mistakes again with the present crisis and prematurely withdraw aid extended to the most fragile elements of the population. It would not do for the number of children living below the poverty line to increase or for the gender pay gap to widen, for workers' rights to be eroded, or for third world countries to be left by the wayside in the vaccination campaigns. If this were allowed to happen, it would be the economic recovery and democracy itself that would be in jeopardy.

Final analogy in this long list, the two most striking crises of modern economic history were allowed to develop as a result of modifications in banking regulations. As a result of ill-conceived deregulation in the periods preceding the 1929 and 2008 crises, borrowers had access to easy money to finance the acquisition of real estate, while there was a deterioration in the quality of collaterals long before the two crises got under way. The crisis of 1929, like the one in 2008, was triggered by substantial defaults on mortgage loans, in turn leading to significant credit losses for the banks.

Chapter 2

Great Depression, Great Recession: Banks Guilty of Triggering the Crisis

The National Banking Act of 1864, whose aim was partly to bring banks under the control of the federal government and thereby set standards of good practice, prohibited any type of lending on real estate (see White, Regulation and Reform). Under the Federal Reserve Act of 1913, conditions were slightly liberalised for country national banks so as to allow them to make farm mortgages for a duration of up to five years, which could not exceed 25% of capital and surplus or a third of time deposits (United States, Federal Reserve Act, p. 25). In September 1916, this act was amended to allow urban banks to make real estate loans of up to one year, though excluding banks located in central reserve cities (Chicago, New York and St Louis) (see Federal Reserve Board, Index-Digest, p. 44). It is only after the passage of the McFadden Act in 1927 that all national banks were allowed to loan on real estate for five years, to an aggregate amount of 50% of their time deposits (see Lloyd, "Government-induced market failure"). There follows that, during the 1920s, commercial loans declined sharply compared with loans for the purchase of real estate and securities. Loans granted at the end of the 1920s had a greater probability of default and foreclosure than those granted a decade before, as collateral requirements were relaxed in the interval. Credit conditions were eased on account of the optimism that prevailed during the Roaring Twenties, when the economy enjoyed a boom and demand for commercial loans was weaker, companies preferring to finance themselves by raising capital on the stock market rather than by taking out bank loans.

Guilty of the Great Depression

The 1929 crisis started with a raft of bank failures. The most dramatic was the failure of the Bank of United States, which could very well have been avoided. Joseph Broderick, New York State Superintendent of Banks, had sponsored various merger plans which would have saved the bank. Federal Reserve Governor George Harrison devised the final reorganisation plan, under which the Bank of United States would have merged with three other financial institutions: Manufacturers Trust, Public National and International Trust. The success seemed so sure that, two days before the bank closed, the Federal Reserve Bank had issued a statement naming proposed directors for the merger. However, at a meeting held at the New York Bank, the representatives of the Clearing House banks decided against a rescue and withdrew from the arrangement whereby they would have subscribed $30 million in new capital funds to the reorganised institution. Joseph Broderick warned them that this was the "most colossal mistake"[1] they had ever made, adding that "its closing would result in the closing of at least ten other banks in the city and that it might even affect the savings banks."[2] Joseph Broderick reminded "them that only two or three weeks before they had rescued two of the largest private bankers of the city and had willingly put up the money needed" and "recalled that only seven or eight years before that they had come to the aid of one of the biggest trust companies in New York, putting up many times the sum needed to save the Bank of United States." Jackson Reynolds, President of the First National Bank and of the Clearing House Association, said that the decision not to go through with the bank's rescue was definitive and that the effect of the closing would be "only local." Joseph Broderick considered "the bank solvent as a going concern and was at a loss to understand the attitude of askance which the Clearing House banks had adopted toward the real estate holdings." History proved him to be largely right: most of the bank's assets were liquidated over the following two years that followed its closing, enabling it to ultimately payoff 83.5% of its adjusted liabilities at its closing on 11 December 1930.

The failure of the Bank of United States was at the origin of the Great Depression, the first global crisis, which in its wake led to the Second World War. It would take decades for Europe to recover through the construction

---

[1] Commercial and Financial Chronicle, 21 May 1932.
[2] *Ibid.*

of the European Union. It was not until the fall of the Berlin Wall, 60 years later, that democratic regimes were reinstated and Europe's geographical boundaries restored to what they were before the Second World War. The human toll from 1929 to 1989 was extremely high. The macabre tally of the deaths attributable to the two European totalitarian regimes of the 20th century shows that Communism shed even more blood than Nazism.

Guilty of the Great Recession

Three decades after the fall of the Berlin Wall, the European Union was caught up in the subprime crisis of 2008, which had its origin in high risk mortgage loans arranged by banks in the United States. The subprime crisis was also triggered by the failure, in the United States, of a systemic bank that could have been rescued.

In the 1990s, subprimes — that is mortgage loans extended to higher-risk borrowers and charging three percentage points above the rate for equivalent maturity Treasury securities — were still a niche market in the United States.

However, between 2001 and 2006, with banks reaching out for yield, subprime mortgages rose sevenfold. This begs the question of why the Federal Reserve did not raise rates as early as 2003 to head off a worst-case scenario.

Delaying a rise in interest rates could be expected to fuel an upward spiral in real estate prices, something Federal Reserve members were well aware of. Nevertheless, for many members, the net social evaluation of the boom in subprime lending was a strong positive as, in less than nine years, monetary policy resulted in 9 million new homeowners, of whom more than half were from ethnic minorities. The overall homeown-ership rate thus increased from 64% in 1994 to more than 68% in 2003.[3]

The problem lay in that new opportunities for homeownership did not stem naturally from an increase in household disposable income, but arti-ficially from the increased availability of credit. Banks prospered by lend-ing to low-income households, many being left destitute after their homes were seized when they could not repay their loans. Millions of Americans lost their homes during the Great Recession. Though this was a real estate crisis, barely $10 billion was provided to struggling homeowners. Yet, at

---

[3] Gramlich, E. (2004) *Subprime Mortgage Lending: Benefits, Costs, and Challenges*, Financial Services Roundtable Annual Housing Policy Meeting, Chicago, Illinois.

the same time, the very banks that precipitated this crisis were rescued by injecting several hundred billion dollars. Foreclosures were decreed against households that had invested all of their savings in their homes, plunging millions of Americans into poverty.

In a tweet published on 17 October 2008 on the Time Magazine website, Nobel laureate Joseph Stiglitz urged the US government to do everything possible to help poor homeowners stay in their homes. The winner of the 2011 Nobel Prize in Economic Sciences wrote, "Too little is being done. We need to help people stay in their homes, by converting the mortgage-interest and property-tax deductions into cashable tax credits; by reforming bankruptcy laws to allow expedited restructuring, which would bring down the value of the mortgage when the price of the house is below that of the mortgage; and even government lending, taking advantage of the government's lower cost of funds and passing the savings on to poor and middle-income homeowners."[4] The federal government ignored his recommendations.

2007 proved a turning point for lower-income Americans. The wealth (difference between a family's assets and debts) of lower-income families was just $9,465 in 2013, 18% less than in 1983. Over the same period, the wealth of middle-income families increased by 2% to $98,057. On the other hand, the wealth of upper-income families had doubled to $650,074 in 2013. There follows that America's upper-income families had a median net worth that was nearly 70 times that of lower-income families and almost seven times that of middle-income families.[5]

These income inequalities played a major role in the crisis. In the first decades after the Second World War, the income of American households increased across all social classes, more strongly at the bottom than at the top of the ladder. Thereafter, while the country's GDP continued to grow, the income of most Americans stagnated. It is always preferable for a country to grow the pie to be shared out, but it must then be divided in slices of such sizes that everyone profits and that the market economy prospers. If not, there will be an excessive concentration of resources in too few hands, contributing to the creation of speculative bubbles that, when they burst, will harm the entire economy.

---

[4] Stiglitz, J. (2008). *Nobel Laureate: How to Get Out of the Financial Crisis*, http://content. time.com/time/business/article/0,8599,1851739-3,00.html.
[5] www.pewsocialtrnds.org/2015/12/09/5-wealth-gap-between-middle-income-and-upper-income-familiesreaches-record-high/.

Strangely enough, the economic assessment by a country's population is not always accurate, but then the lack of transparency on the politicians' part does tend to stack the cards. For example, it is astonishing that President Bill Clinton should have remained the most popular president of the United States, even though it was during his term of office that the Glass–Steagall Act was repealed, leading to the subprime crisis.

The Glass–Steagall Act was passed within days of President Franklin Roosevelt taking office in March 1933 in the aftermath of the Great Depression. This legislation can be traced back to the policy pursued at the turn of the century by a distant relative, President Teddy Roosevelt, who sought to break up powerful trusts, adjudged to be too big to fail and guilty therefore of taking disproportionate risks.

A few years after the 2008 crisis, the American middle class had still not come to the realisation that the deterioration in the economic situation was due to the crisis and not globalisation, nor was it aware that politicians had been rather coy about their responsibility for the subprime crisis. Doubtless politicians felt they had nothing to gain from explaining the causes of this extremely serious crisis and its short- to medium-term effects.

The federal government allowed Lehman Brothers to fail even though this bank presented a systemic risk, and it then failed to support the real estate sector, despite its role in triggering the crisis. Because of these two errors, the economic recovery was not vigorous enough to stem the rise of populism.

The election of Donald Trump dealt a blow to the international liberal economic order constructed by the United States after the Second World War. As President of the United States, Donald Trump applied himself to dismantling the world order based on multilateralism established at Bretton Woods in 1944, and which had brought economic growth and alleviated poverty thanks to the boom in global trade. Yet, globalisation was not what exacerbated inequalities in the United States. The deterioration in the economic situation of Trump's electorate was brought about by the economic consequences of the subprime crisis and a fuelling of income inequality that failed to be corrected by an efficient social and fiscal system. President Joe Biden is trying to put things right, but his success remains to be assessed.

Chapter 3

COVID-19 Crisis: Banks Have the Capacity to Finance Recovery

Health emergency or crisis of the healthcare system?

Unlike the great crises of the past, or at least those of the recent past which everyone remembers and looks to in trying to overcome present difficulties, the economic crisis into which the whole world was plunged in 2020 does not have a financial origin. Its dynamics are different, not only because the development of an epidemic has its own, very specific mechanisms but also because the economic impact is very different from that of any other type of crisis. We have looked in detail at the mechanisms at work in the great global crises of 1929 and 2008. With COVID-19, however, economic life is being disrupted in a very unusual way, and this needs to be analysed to find the right remedy.

The first new element, at least not seen for over a century, is that the world faced an unknown human disease that affects everyone.

It was unknown, not because those who first experienced it downplayed its importance, but because, even when all the scientists in the world turned their attention to this emerging infection, with the very substantial resources that everyone quickly made available to them, they did not immediately find the mechanism at work in the transmission of this virus or in its effect on patients. Highly contradictory instructions were issued, in the form of general infection prevention and control (IPC) measures, combined with specific measures such as the opening and closing of schools (which varied over time and from one country to the next). This showed that, at the start of the outbreak, nobody really knew how this virus was transmitted. When the first patients were admitted, a multitude of treatments were tried by doctors. There not being necessarily any scientific certainty, much depended on the personality of the treating doctor, some being convinced these treatments would have therapeutic benefits, when others proceeded more cautiously. Hucksters and charlatans were quick to join in this cacophony, in a sort of improvised theatre in white coats, where the President of the United States himself took to the stage as an extra. This would be laughable if it did not reveal how helpless we are in the face of uncertainty. This stupefaction is undoubtedly the undesirable effect of humanity's immense progress in the field of science in the last century or two. We have become accustomed to each problem falling within a clearly identified field and having at least one solution, with its advantages and weaknesses, with flaws therefore, but which are known, quantified. For both the man in the street and the minister in charge, not having the foggiest idea of what was happening was very destabilising. Though vaccines were developed in next to no time, and treatment protocols have gradually led to the emergence of ways of caring for seriously ill patients, the anxiety of staring into the unknown remains. Beware: fear is of poor counsel.

Another element that has not been experienced in our lifetime is that not only did the pandemic strike everywhere but that everyone could be affected. There have been new, deadly infectious diseases before, which could not be prevented or cured, but they were endemic to a geographic area or population group. At the onset, AIDS seemed to only affect homosexuals. The Ebola disease is wreaking havoc and causing panic, but occurs primarily on the African continent. Analogies could be drawn with SARS, a distant cousin of COVID-19, but the outbreak was largely confined to Asia. It is easy to see how, in these cases, general anxiety is dulled. This is quite otherwise with COVID-19: everyone is at risk of infection and, although the elderly are the least resistant to the virus, young apparently healthy patients are also succumbing. When was the last time humanity experienced a phenomenon on this scale, invisible, incomprehensible and indiscriminate? The Middle Ages, perhaps, with the plague that inspired Jean de La Fontaine's famous "They died not all, but all were sick."[1]

---

[1] La Fontaine, Jean de (1678) *Les animaux malades de la peste*. English translation by Wright, Elizur Jr. (1842) *The Fables of La Fontaine, The Animals Sick of the Plague*, pp. 39–40, retrieved from the Internet Archive.

The COVID-19 pandemic is the most serious pandemic of the past century. In Europe, the initial wave first affected Italy, Spain, the Netherlands, Sweden and the United Kingdom. By August 2020, the virus had spread to the whole of Europe at such speed that it already seemed the continent was ailing, left weaker and frailer.

Although Europeans would argue that they live their life according to the precept "a healthy mind in a healthy body", it would seem that leading a healthier life is challenging in the best of times. Then, there is the fact that the 2008 and COVID-19 crises heightened certain behaviours detrimental to health.

> "Research shows that people experiencing financial difficulties are at greater risk of obesity, and that this risk increases with the severity and recurrence of these difficulties. Research conducted in Germany, Finland and the United Kingdom shows that there is a causal effect between financial distress and obesity. The economic crisis is thus contributing to an increase in the number of obese people in Europe, which can no longer be explained solely by a lack of physical activity and the consumption of foods too rich in fat, sugar and salt."[2]

The rise in the number of overweight people reflects the rise in poverty. There are major socio-economic disparities when it comes to obesity. The proportion of overweight and obese children is twice as high in the families with the lowest incomes. As wealth becomes increasingly concentrated, the number of overweight and obese people increases. There follows that poor people are disproportionately affected by the pandemic, as obesity is a recognised predisposing factor for complications arising from COVID-19 infections.

So, we need to ask ourselves what the state of health of the French population was when the COVID-19 virus began to spread in the country. Were there any risk factors that amplified the COVID-19 health crisis in France? Undeniably, yes: the country was older and more tired than its neighbours when the virus struck.

The public transport strike that preceded the COVID-19 crisis had a debilitating effect on the general population, therefore on healthcare staff, in particular nurses, who were exhausted by the time the pandemic struck.

---

[2] www.challenges.fr/tribunes/comment-la-crise-economiqueimpacte-la-sante-des-europeens_129953.

The Yellow Vest movement, just before the transport strike, had also been very psychologically taxing for high street retailers.

Generally speaking, unlike the Spanish flu, the COVID-19 virus has had a serious impact mainly on the elderly. In 2020, according to the European Union and the OECD, in almost all countries, at least 90% of deaths linked to COVID-19 involved people aged 60 and over. In France, the proportion of the population aged over 60 has risen steadily, from 16.4% in 2007 to 19.8% in 2018. The residents of retirement homes were particularly exposed to the COVID-19 virus. Mortality statistics in the first months of the pandemic understated COVID-related deaths since they did not include deaths at retirement homes.

As COVID-19 affects the lungs, smoking is a risk factor. Despite an increasingly dissuasive tax system and the ban on smoking in enclosed spaces, surveys found that 25.4% of French people smoked every day in 2018. This was down from 29.7% in 2010, but this is surpassed in only two OECD countries: Greece and Russia. In the European Union, smoking remains the most significant cause of premature death, responsible for nearly 700,000 deaths a year. The fact that a quarter of the French population continues to smoke in the 21st century underlines the inadequacy of preventive measures in this area.

In France, more is invested in curative treatment than in preventive measures. And yet, investment in prevention would be so much better in term of health outcomes and would be far more cost effective for the population and the state than curative treatment! Of course, the pharmaceutical industry would lose out, but society as a whole would benefit. If people are in good health, less will be spent on expensive treatments (whether through private care or through the social security system, the costs being passed on in taxes and/or social security contributions), taxes will be less, dissatisfaction with the power in place be will will be less and temptations to turn to the extremes will be less.

Another health policy failure is obesity. This was a risk factor during the COVID-19 pandemic, associated with progressions to severe COVID-19 in adults. In the European Union, more than one adult in six is obese. While France continues to pride itself on the fact that health is in what people find on their plate, 49% of the French population aged over 15 is overweight or obese. While there may be some comfort that it is higher in many countries, the direction taken by France is alarming. In the thousand years that France has existed as a nation, this is the first time that one French person in two has been overweight! Only Japan, an even older nation, is bucking the global obesity trend, with only 26.7% of its population overweight.

COVID-19 having found susceptible hosts, the portal of entry was wide open. With half the population overweight or obese, the scale of the health crisis increased tenfold. The Spanish flu could not have thrived on the terrain of obesity, but that was more than a century ago: since then, the human body has undergone a major change. Enslaved by Zeus, it is now an overweight Atlas who must hold up the earth on his shoulders for all eternity. Weakened by COVID-19, the Titan stumbles and the world with him.

> "The correlation between the high concentration of fine particles and the severity of influenza waves is well known to epidemiologists. An interdisciplinary team from the University of Geneva (UNIGE) and the ETH Zürich spin-off Meteodat investigated possible interactions between acutely elevated levels of fine particulate matter and the virulence of the coronavirus disease. Their results, published in the journal Earth Systems and Environment, suggest that high concentrations of particles less than 2.5 micrometers in size may modulate, or even amplify, the waves of SARS-CoV-2 contamination and explain in part the particular profile of the COVID-19 pandemic."[3]

Thus, as researcher Antoine Flahault stated,[4] the third wave of the COVID-19 epidemic, which led to the third lockdown in March 2021, can be explained in part by the pollution and increase in fine particles experienced at the start of 2021. In his view, reducing air pollution could limit future surges in morbidity and mortality due to the coronavirus.

"The economic and welfare losses from air pollution are substantial. New estimates of the impact of $PM_{2.5}$ and ozone show that losses amounted to about €600 billion in 2017 or 4.9% of gross domestic product (GDP) across the EU as a whole. This is due mainly to the impact these air pollutants have on mortality, but also to the lower quality of life and labour productivity for people living with related diseases, and higher health expenditure."[5] Between 2005 and 2017, fine particle emissions fell

---

[3] https://www.unige.ch/medias/en/2020/covid-19-la-qualite-de-lair-influence-la-pandemie.
[4] C dans l'air, France 5, March 2021.
[5] OECD/European Union (2020), *Health at a Glance: Europe 2020: State of Health in the EU Cycle*, p. 14.

in OECD countries. Nevertheless, the emission levels remain a health hazard and amplify the spread of COVID-19 by weakening the lungs.

So, it is not surprising that there are more serious cases of COVID-19 in the capital cities than in other regions. The level of fine particles is highest there. Although this level has fallen since 2013, it often remains above the limit recommended by the World Health Organization (WHO).[6] Admittedly, several capital cities such as Stockholm, Tallinn, Helsinki, Dublin, Oslo and Luxembourg are below the $PM_{2.5}$ level set by Organization. In Paris, on the other hand, the level of fine particles is well above the WHO limit and above the level in other major cities such as Rome, Amsterdam, Brussels, Vilnius, Copenhagen, Lisbon, London and Madrid. Many countries have dramatically reduced their per capita $PM_{2.5}$ emissions. The best pupils in the class are the Netherlands, Malta and Switzerland, which halved their emissions between 2005 and 2017. They are closely followed by the United Kingdom, Austria, Sweden, Lithuania and Luxembourg.

COVID-19 revealed not only the frailties of 21st century Man but also those of healthcare systems. The pandemic put the spotlight on public health, which finally became a political priority once again after years of budget cuts. When confronted by the COVID-19 pandemic, Europe's healthcare systems were found to be wanting, to the great astonishment of Europeans. What emerged, in France, was that the number of intensive care beds had fallen sharply since 2007, from 3.6 beds per 1,000 inhabitants in 2007 to 3 beds in 2018. In fact, France had been below the OECD average of 4.7 hospital beds per 1,000 inhabitants ever since 2007. The disparities at country level are striking: in Japan and Korea, the figure is 13.1 and 12.3, respectively. Closer to home, Germany has 8 beds per 1,000 inhabitants and Austria 7.4.

In other words, it is the French healthcare system that paid the price for the financial crisis. Savings were made in an area that is, quite literally, a vital organ of the state. The deterioration in the general population's health following the 2008 crisis was thus accompanied by a deterioration in the healthcare system. Under these conditions, was there any other solution than to lock down the entire country to cope with the COVID-19 pandemic? Could the home of Louis Pasteur, so proud of its hospitals, be satisfied with a solution harking back to the Middle Ages? Even back

---

[6]European Environment Agency Air Quality Statistics database, 2020 — www.eea.europa. eu/data-and-maps/dashboards/air-quality-statistics-expert-viewer.

then, there were no nationwide lockdowns to deal with epidemics! Never before had Paris been locked down: a first that is anything but a step forward. The financial and human cost of the successive lockdowns will certainly exceed what it would have cost to maintain a healthcare system worthy of France. Sadly, we all know of at least one hospital that has closed in the last decade. This pandemic has highlighted the shortage of healthcare professionals and the country's dependence on imports for critical health supplies.

As patients admitted to intensive care units have a mortality rate of about 30%, the long-term objective should not just be to increase the number of intensive care beds. A healthier population would make it possible to avoid serious forms of COVID-19, as well as other diseases. It is therefore vital to invest more in preventive medicine to support the population, not wait for the next health emergency. In the immediate aftermath of the 2008 financial crisis, there was a dramatic fall in the number of doctors in France. The number did rise slightly from 2010 onwards so that France had 3.37 doctors for every 1,000 people in 2018. This is insufficient to dispense both preventive and curative medicine. As doctors find themselves providing emergency treatment, they have to concentrate on what is most urgent, curative medicine. As an old proverbial saying dating back to the start of the 17th century goes, "Prevention is better than cure". Do we have the psychological and financial resources to wait another four centuries before applying this fundamental principle of modern healthcare?

In Pasteur's homeland, the institute that bears his name has been unable to compete in terms of investment with its American and German competitors to produce a vaccine. This is part of an underlying trend, as the percentage of GDP devoted to research and development is 2.2% in France, compared with over 3% in Germany and the United States. What's more, France's GDP is also lower. In 2019, France's GDP was $2.716 billion, Germany's was $3.861 billion and the United States' was $21.43 trillion. Given the amount spent on research and development, it goes without saying that France can no longer win the vaccine race alone, as it has done in the past.

China, where the crisis began, and countries that produced vaccines, such as the United States and the United Kingdom, were the first to defeat the pandemic thanks to sufficiently large-scale vaccination campaigns. They experienced a strong economic recovery and captured market share, while countries importing vaccines, masks and resuscitation equipment had no choice but to remain locked down, waiting their turn to import the required doses. They were left watching the train of economic growth go by with their competitors on board. They slipped down the world order, and the influence of their culture worldwide faded. There is every reason to believe that France is going to rack and ruin, losing ground in the global economy, because of a lack of interest in a field in which it has been a leader for a century. Admittedly, the country could still have excellent researchers, were it not for the fact they have to exile themselves to fund their research.

Economic crisis or crisis of an economic system?

Besides the public health and psychological shocks, the second very different aspect of this crisis has been its economic impact, this being a propagated source epidemic. To curb the transmission of the virus, human interactions had to be reduced. Governments everywhere took steps to this end. The method chosen was crude, with many drawbacks, but there was no alternative while waiting for vaccines and cures. One of the drawbacks has been the hugely negative and highly specific impact on the economy.

To reduce human interactions, shops were ordered to close or opening hours were restricted. Entire sectors of the economy were affected. This meant a lower footfall for retailers, shop assistants being placed on furlough, fewer orders being placed with suppliers, which in turn scaled back their activity, unpaid bills, affecting creditors, and outstanding loans and interest, affecting banks. When restaurants were closed, farmers and fishermen had no outlet for their produce. When the curtain fell on theatres, cinemas and concert halls, they immediately ceased to generate any revenue. Most of them had been in precarious financial health for a long time, so it was easy to anticipate the fallout. Economic activity started to grind to a halt everywhere, from the high streets to the factories. There were few winners save for businesses providing goods or services without physical contact. They were quickly accused of being profiteers, when in fact they were no more responsible for the situation than brick-and-mortar retailers ordered to close up shop. All in all, unfortunately, there have been far fewer winners than losers, with the economy left barely ticking over.

In every country, governments set up programmes to support the economy. In France, it was Emmanuel Macron's famous "whatever the cost". Unemployment benefits went some way towards compensating for the loss of salary for employees furloughed because their business had been temporarily shut down or they had to stay at home to look after their children during school closures. Civil servants, too, continued to be paid even when their workload had shrunk. Retired people, of whom there are many in Western countries where people live to a ripe old age, are another category whose income was not affected. All in all, according to INSEE, the average purchasing power of French people in 2020 remained stable,[7] a situation unprecedented in a crisis of this magnitude.

The crisis was therefore characterised by a highly atypical situation: household income was largely preserved, but consumption opportunities were severely suppressed, leading to forced savings. Never has there been so much money in bank accounts. Never, moreover, were there so many scam attempts, with fraudsters always a leading indicator of changes underway, agility being a prerequisite to stay ahead of the game. But, above all, these accumulated savings offer some hope for the recovery. It could be all the faster in that there could be some form of catching-up in consumption. It is also a possible source of funding for future investment, provided that the right mechanism can be found to reassure savers about the soundness of the risk taken when investing their savings. The means of achieving this are well known: diversification of investments, selection by risk professionals and coverage of initial losses by the state or private funds. French savers being traditionally exceedingly risk-averse, their reaction to these measures is more uncertain. Mechanisms will undoubtedly have to be tweaked as the situation evolves. Banks, whose historic role and recognised expertise is precisely to transform savings (often those of private individuals) into financing (often provided to businesses or governments), obviously have an essential role to play to avoid unfortunate outcomes.

Those worst affected were the ones who derived their income directly from their work: shopkeepers, self-employed, temporary workers, seasonal workers and undeclared workers. With the exception of the latter, governments have tried to find ways of helping these economic agents get by. It has been a question of sitting it out as long as possible until the pandemic is brought under control.

Having considered the fate of households (fairly well protected financially in France) and businesses (kept rather artificially on life support until they could get going again), one word about states. They are the ones

---

[7]Calignon, Guillaume de (2021) *Covid: malgré la crise, le pouvoir d'achat moyen des Français n'a pas reculé en 2020*. Les Echos, 26 February 2021.

absorbing most of the cost of this economic crisis, and France is no exception. The risk posed by the huge debt accumulated in the process will be examined later.

The situation of businesses is certainly far more perilous than that of households. The fall in household consumption affects all businesses that produce goods and services other than basic necessities. Not having been spent, the money is in personal bank accounts, not in business bank accounts. Restriction measures (travel bans, curfews and lockdowns) made it difficult or impossible for their employees to come to work, reducing their production capacity. As the crisis is global, their supply chains are affected, even when they had taken care to diversify their suppliers, creating an additional obstacle to their smooth operation. Faced with all these obstacles, and fearing a proliferation of bankruptcies, governments took action. In France, bankers were the first to act, offering their customers affected by the crisis a systematic moratorium, deferring loan repayments until the situation became clearer. Whether in activity or not, businesses needed cash to meet fixed costs. As a rule, in many countries, this came out of the public purse. In France, a system of state-guaranteed loans was set up, enabling banks to release up to three months' sales while bearing only 10% of the risk in the event the borrower defaulted, the other 90% being borne ultimately by the state. This massive operation was implemented in record time, with the banks toiling night and day to draw up the contracts and modify processing chains, all the while working remotely. In six months, more than €100 billion was released.

One surprising effect of this crisis is that banks have never worked so hard. Like all companies, they were called upon to adapt their systems to remote working without allowing this to affect their operations. Banking was one of the few economic sectors for which continued operations were considered to be vitally important, whatever the circumstances. But, they have also been at pains to meet the challenges of the moment, supporting customers in their time of need. They accelerated the rollout of remote banking services and contactless payment, provided retail customers with the payment terminals and sometimes the e-commerce sites they needed to keep their businesses going, sped up payments to their small suppliers and set up the famous moratoria and state-guaranteed loans for a great many customers. Unlike in previous crises, banks have seen their business grow rather than shrink. Another notable difference is that they have not had to deal, at least not yet, with a wave of bankruptcies among their customers. Curiously singled out for keeping their branches open across the country, they have done what they know best: provide customers with financial solutions on a timely basis.

Crisis management focused on reducing social interactions as much as possible, bringing about a brutal U-turn in our society. For decades, society had been developing to the rhythm of exchanges in the professional sphere as well as in private life: ever more contacts, with ever more interlocutors, in ever more varied places, at ever greater distances. Just think of the latest trend talked about before Wuhan: moving from an ownership society to a leasing society, where access is more important than ownership, for example, borrowing a car or a bike for an errand or a weekend, house swapping to enjoy a change of scenery or household equipment that can be supplied by a specialist for a monthly fee and replaced on a whim. The traditional offices, in which desks are assigned to particular employees, are disappearing in both the private and public sectors, replaced increasingly by flexible workspace. All this implied physical interactions, sharing objects and therefore the possibility of infection. IPC measures came as a slap in the face of the smiley-face society, forced to don a mask, while outstretched hands were replaced by elbow bumps.

Chapter 4

Banks: The Cornerstone of the Recovery?

Since they are not one of the causes of the crisis that is unfolding, which was the result of an epidemic, banks have every capacity to play a leading role in resolving the economic fallout. In this, they are part of the long tradition that has made them essential players in reconstruction efforts after wars or natural disasters, in driving expansion after the periods of self-isolation imposed by certain governments and in assisting development when populations have been freed from the yoke of repressive regimes. There would have been no Trente Glorieuses in France, no poverty alleviation in China and no economic emancipation of women in South Asia had it not been for banks, large and small, providing the funds that unleashed pent-up energies.

The situation of banks at a time when economies have been hardest hit by the COVID-19 crisis is such that they can be directly involved in the recovery effort.

First, since the Great Recession, own funds have been rebuilt to very considerable levels by banks at the prompting of regulators, financial analysts and, sometimes, their shareholders. Even though bank balance sheets, as measured by total assets, have grown significantly over the last decade, own funds have grown even more markedly, so that the solvency of banks has more than doubled on average. As a result, banks have the reserves they need to meet the cost of the risk on any advances and loans not ultimately repaid by certain debtors and to provide sufficient new loans to get the economic apparatus back in gear. In financial terms, therefore, banks have the necessary resources to participate in the recovery plans in the countries where they operate.

This did not escape governments, which were quick to find ways of leveraging these private resources to amplify their effect and speed up the economic recovery. Across Europe, the staging of central bank refinancing operations (TLTROs in the euro area) helped to mitigate the liquidity risk of banks, which would go on to play their part by increasing lending to the economy. In France, state-guaranteed loans had the effect of limiting to a modest share the credit risk exposure of banks taking part in this scheme. Under the subordinated loan scheme to support enterprises through the crisis, first losses were picked up by the state, allowing bankers and insurers to provide debt financing while enjoying a degree of protection, these investments naturally being riskier than operations in the normal course of business. In both cases, Emmanuel Macron's "whatever the cost" was applied with a focus on efficiency, meaning that amounts committed by the state were leveraged though the intervention of the banks, suddenly reassured.

Another factor supporting decisive intervention by the banks is that the people most seriously affected by the economic crisis are, among their customers, those most heavily indebted and therefore those they know best. This is true of personal customers, who have been relatively less affected in France thanks to the pre-existing safety net, which was strengthened under the "whatever the cost" policy. The same is true of their corporate customers, who are traditionally more indebted than private individuals and who in some sectors have seen their revenues wiped out and their losses literally soar. Given emergency measures taken to defer the impact of these bankruptcies, it is impossible to measure the full extent of the damage, but it will certainly be considerable.

This is even truer of their professional customers, who were particularly affected by the lockdowns and curfews. With each of these customers, the bank will have a personal relationship, built up over the years, enabling it to understand their specific situation, vulnerabilities and prospects. Banks have given commitments to each of these customers, and bringing these to a successful conclusion will be a legitimate concern in their eyes. Consequently, with each of these customers, it is in the banks' best interests to find a solution that will ultimately enable them to restart their business and gradually repay their debts. The situation is one where the interests of the state, acting for the common good, borrowers and bankers are one.

Every cloud has a silver lining. The very weak consumption by the entire population as a result of infection prevention and control (IPC) measures led to a pronounced increase in the bank balances of most personal customers. All the more resources were available to banks that could be channelled into the economy. The general movement of solidarity in favour of shopkeepers and small businesses is also manifesting itself with renewed vigour at this critical time for them. Crowdfunding platforms, an area in which banks are also involved, will also make it possible to channel some of the public's savings towards small businesses in need of capital.

Another consequence of the lockdowns and curfews has been the accelerated adoption of new methods of consumption and, therefore, payment. For banks, this was an opportunity to speed up the rollout of remote or contactless payment solutions, as well as the installation of software at the premises of business customers, including shopkeepers, to adapt to the remote selling of services or goods, with or without the use of "click and collect". Following in the footsteps of some municipal and local authorities, banks have begun providing customers, particularly those directly affected by the COVID-19 crisis, with solutions enabling them to do business differently and adapt to the new environment.

All in all, in a closely coordinated effort with the public sector under the aegis of central banks and governments, banks in major developed countries have been in a position to provide not only financial but also very practical responses to the difficulties encountered by business customers (including shopkeepers and self-employed professionals) and by personal customers as a result of the health crisis and resulting restrictions of all kinds. This is a major difference from previous crises, and will do much to speed the economic recovery. It is the only way to rapidly turn the page on two years that have wreaked havoc on the physical and psychological well-being of the population and on the economy.

Part II

In the Cold Light of Day

Νεμεσις[*]

In Greek mythology, Nemesis was the goddess who personified divine wrath, or retribution for the sin of hubris: pride, insolence or arrogance before the gods. She could be born from the ocean, like storms, or from the night, like nightmares. Is it not Nemesis who seems to emerge after the all-too-human excesses, after the hubris, or the wild abandon and excessive self-confidence that caused the Great Depression early on in the 20th century, and then the Great Recession almost a century later? Is it not Nemesis who manifests herself in the aftermath of crises, in the cold light of day, when the world awakens to a harsh reality?

---

[*]The term refers to the Greek goddess of vengeance, the personification of divine wrath, punishment for hubris. The Greek hubris referred to presumption towards the gods, everything in man's behaviour considered by the gods as wanton violence, insolence, outrage. Hubris generally precedes crises, and unfortunately is invariably followed by Nemesis.

Chapter 5

France: Centuries of History … and of Debt

France's sovereign debt scaled new heights after the Great Recession and COVID-19 crisis. Were these a first? Is this debt spiral worrying? How did France break out from this spiral in the past?

The earliest year for which there is a surviving written record of the word for debt in French is 1160. The word debt comes from the Latin "debitum", which means "thing owed". The French word for "indebtedness" appears in 1611. The French words for "overindebted" and "overindebtedness" appear in 1985 to express a new economic and financial reality according to Alain Rey.

The definition of overindebtedness for individuals differs in each country, as do remedies, such as insolvency proceedings and debt discharge. In the event of overindebtedness, continental European countries find it more difficult than Anglo-Saxon countries to write off debts to allow a fresh start. But, even in Anglo-Saxon countries, the debts of middle-class individuals are not treated in the same way as those of high-net-worth individuals and governments. As the American industrialist Jean Paul Getty once said, "If you owe the bank $100, that's your problem. If you owe the bank $100 million, that's the bank's problem."

In France, the procedure for dealing with overindebtedness, designed to provide solutions for households in financial difficulty, is 30 years old. It was implemented following the promulgation of Law no. 89-1010 of 31 December 1989, known as the Neiertz law. In France, 4.5 million overindebtedness applications have been submitted since the law was passed, equivalent to 155,000 a year.[1] While the treatment of overindebtedness is recent, as suggested by the word's etymology, this is not a new phenomenon.

Credulity is the starting point: from believers persuaded to buy indulgences from the Church as "a remission before God of the temporal punishment due to sins whose guilt has already been forgiven"[2] to people who could not afford to become homeowners being coaxed into taking out subprime loans, the historical development of the idea of debt has seen many twists and turns. Did the sinners go to paradise? Who's to say, but what is sure is that one-third of households having taken out a subprime loan between 2005 and 2007 to buy their home could not repay it. Whether it was the Church or the banks, they got off scot-free. The 2008 crisis upset the international economic order, exacerbated inequalities and triggered a rise of populism and protectionism around the world. Nevertheless, more than a decade on, rarely have legal proceedings been instituted against creditors.

However, throughout history, the fate of creditors has not always been enviable, particularly when lending to the strong and mighty. Sometimes, the methods used to cancel France's sovereign debt have been quite extreme. At the start of the 14th century, France's creditors were burned at the stake by Philippe IV to fill the kingdom's empty coffers. At that time, the Knights Templar lent money with or without interest, depending on the sum, and had become a financial power in Europe. On 13 October 1307, Philippe IV had all the Knights Templar in France arrested and all their assets, amassed during the Crusades, confiscated. These assets were entrusted to the custody of the National Treasury. The Inquisition accused the knights of idolatry and heresy. They were tortured until they admitted the charges or died. With their demise, the king cancelled all the debts owed to the Order and seized all their possessions.

Unfortunately, the French monarchy remained chronically indebted. Sovereign debt dynamics under Louis XIV remained a feature in subsequent centuries, right up to the present day. In the early years of the reign, attempts were made to contain the debt, but it grew exponentially and eventually got out of hand.

---

[1] Banque de France (2019), *Overindebtedness and women*, Bulletin no. 224: Article 3.
[2] Vatican, *Catechism of the Catholic Church*, https://www.vatican.va/archive/ENG0015/__P4G.HTM.

When Cardinal Mazarin died in 1661, Louis XIV refused to appoint a Chief Minister. Shortly after, Colbert helped the King get rid of Nicolas Fouquet, Superintendent of Finances, and took his place, but was never given the title. As Pierre Goubert explains in his book, *Louis XIV et vingt millions de Français*,[3] Mazarin had increased "les comptants", i.e. discretionary spending by the King, to 100 million livres. On his death, the tax receipts of 1661, 1662 and part of the receipts of 1663 had already been spent in advance. A Chamber of Justice was set up in 1661 to investigate all malfeasance committed since 1635. Indictments were often based on denunciation. Fundholders and small lenders were most often the victims of this ad hoc court. In eight years, 110 million livres — the equivalent of a year and a half of tax receipts — were raised in this way.

In his first twelve years in office, Jean-Baptiste Colbert excelled, slashing the state's spending. According to French historian Pierre Goubert, spending, which was in majority borne by the population of Paris, was cut from 52 million livres to 24 million livres in ten years. The tax base was expanded by rescinding tax exemptions. Fees paid to tax farmers were cut from 25% to 4%. Not only did Colbert tighten up the management of public finances but he also pursued an aggressive customs policy, following in the footsteps of Cardinal Mazarin.

The Compagnie française pour le commerce des Indes orientales was started in 1664 to develop trade. Its creation was shortly before the introduction in 1667 of a new customs tariff designed to discourage imports of Dutch goods in favour of French goods. As Dutch drapes and fabric were highly sought after, Jean-Baptiste Colbert transferred the entire Maincy workshop in 1662 to a Parisian faubourg where the small Bièvre River flowed through a district called Les Gobelins, the Crown going on to install and fund the Royal Manufactory of Crown Furnishings at the Gobelins.[4] Colbert also subsidised some twenty other manufactories, arsenals and shipyards. In the pursuit of his protectionist policy, he encouraged French products in place of imported products. The development of these ventures and their aura, first in France and then further afield, instilled confidence in France over the medium term. Some of these companies have survived to this day, and over the centuries paid handsome dividends to the Crown and then the state.

---

[3] Goubert, P. (2010). *Louis XIV et vingt millions de Français*. Pluriel.
[4] In French, Manufacture royale des meubles de la Couronne aux Gobelins.

In 1672, Louis XIV went to war against Holland, with the result that public spending exceeded receipts. The deficit reached more than 8 million livres and continued to grow, reaching 24 million livres in 1676. Colbert wrote to Louis XIV, "Your Majesty has never consulted his finances to decide on his expenditures." He added that "the administration of one's finances, profuse with details, is not the natural and ordinary occupation of kings."[5] Colbert was forced to borrow from Genoese bankers, who charged interest at 10%. In 1676, for example, he secured an advance equivalent to the 1677 tax receipts plus a further 15 million livres. As France was more or less constantly at war during the next two decades, the debt continued to balloon. In his book,[6] Pierre Goubert explains that, at the death of Louis XIV in 1715, Nicolas Desmarets, the Controller-General of Finances, estimated the Crown had net receipts of 74 million livres for 119 million of expenditures. The total debt had spiralled to 2 billion livres, of which 400 million livres was payable on demand. Future crown receipts were assigned to the benefit of creditors, in the form of promissory notes issued by a credit institution, Caisse des Emprunts, established to sustain the war effort. These notes circulated at deep discounts alongside a currency having undergone a series of debasements.

In his book, *De Louis XVI à Napoléon*,[7] Jean Tulard explains that, when Louis XVI came to the throne in 1774, there was a 335 million livres hole in the crown coffers. Although the concept of gross domestic product (GDP) dates back to the 17th century, until the French Revolution, the analysis of public finance was not based on measuring public debt as a percentage of GDP but on comparing public debt against tax receipts. In 1774, the Crown had spent in advance 78 million livres of future tax receipts. Expressed as a percentage of GDP, the public debt ratio reached 60% when the French Revolution broke out. Nothing shocking about this by current standards, but there is one big difference, being that fiscal administration was far less efficient under the Ancient Regime than it is now.

Abbot Joseph Marie Terray, who served as Louis XV's last Controller-General of Finances, advised the new king to declare a national bankruptcy. This was a momentous decision for the new monarch, who was just 19, and he baulked at this.

---

[5] Goubert, P. (2010) *Louis XIV et vingt millions de Français*. Pluriel.
[6] *Ibid.*
[7] Tulard, J. (1995) *De Louis XVI à Napoléon*. Le Grand Livre du mois.

Louis XVI preferred the counsel of Anne Robert Jacques Turgot, who was appointed Controller-General of Finances two months after the king's accession. He recommended stimulating growth by instituting free trade, notably of grains, and abolishing guilds to encourage innovations. These reforms aroused a great deal of discontent among the major beneficiaries of the established order. The Controller-General of Finances also antagonised courtiers, having obtained from Louis XVI a reduction of 24 million livres in the pensions paid to them by the Crown. Turgot's logic is easy to understand if one considers that the ordinary deficit reached 22 million livres. This led to remonstrances by the Parliament of Paris, which refused to register the reforms, as they were counter to the interests of those enjoying exclusive privileges. On 12 May 1776, Turgot was dismissed just as he was about to enshrine the equality principle in taxation. His reforms would never be implemented.

Turgot was replaced by Jacques Necker, a Geneva banker. He had extensive recourse to loans, not just because this was his area of expertise but also because support for the American War of Independence cost 1 billion livres. To be able to borrow, Necker had to publish a statement of the Crown's receipts and expenditures[8] for 1781. Lenders were not reassured on discovering that the spending on the court was put at 28 million livres, or as much as on the French Navy. The crown coffers were now empty.

Necker's successors did nothing to rein back the public debt. Tax receipts paid for the lavish entertainment put on for the King and his court at Versailles. Paradoxically, lenders were reassured by the splendour of Versailles and agreed to lend the Crown 487 million livres over three years. The fact that the king was destitute came to light in August 1788 when the Crown was forced to suspend payments.

At the outbreak of the French Revolution, a member of the Third Estate paid 57% tax on his revenues. As for the accumulated deficit, it reached a staggering 2 billion livres.

To absorb the debt as much as to promote equality between the three classes or estates of the realm, the Estates General put an end to tax privileges. To resolve the 2 billion livres accumulated deficit, Charles-Maurice de Talleyrand-Périgord, the then Bishop of Autun, proposed appropriating

---

[8]*Compte rendu au roi*, the first public budget to be released by the Crown. White, E. N. (1995). *The French Revolution and the Politics of Government Finance, 1770–1815*, The Journal of Economic History, 55(2), 227–255.

and selling the properties of the French Church. Promissory notes[9] secured on the properties of the Church were immediately issued to fund the Crown's expenditures. Against the advice of Talleyrand, Honoré Gabriel Riqueti, Count of Mirabeau, transformed these orders to pay into fiat money, which would be issued in vast quantities. In six years, France issued 45 billion livres! At the end of 1797, the Directoire opted for partial bankruptcy, euphemistically referred to as "consolidated third", because it cancelled two-thirds of the sovereign debt. As Jean Tulard explains, Napoleon did his best to avoid resorting to borrowing and endeavoured to keep a balanced budget even in wartime, having witnessed first-hand how the Ancien Régime was brought to its knees by debt.

---

[9] *Assignats.*

Chapter 6

Out of the Great Depression into a World War

Napoleon's empire came crumbling down on the battlefield, defeated by the Quadruple Alliance formed by the then Great Powers of Austria, Britain, Prussia and Russia. Human losses due to the Napoleonic Wars ran into several millions in Europe, of which one million were French.[1] The spoliations that accompanied the Napoleonic campaigns constituted "the greatest art theft in history."[2] Napoleon's defeat also sounded the death knell for the influence of Latin civilisation over Europe, which began almost two millenaries earlier with the Roman Empire. Napoleon would be the last Latin emperor in every sense of the word. Britain would emerge stronger from the war. For his first exile in 1814, Napoleon chose a Mediterranean island; 60 years later, in similar circumstances, his nephew Napoleon III chose England. Since then, the Anglo-Saxon vision of the world has increasingly imposed itself in Latin countries, even more so as a result of two world wars and more recently due to the expansion of the GAFAM and the likes of Netflix. For a century now, Latin has definitively given way to English as the universal language.

After the partial settlements reached at the Treaty of Paris signed on 30 May 1814, a series of diplomatic meetings were held in 1814 and 1815, known collectively as the Congress of Vienna, aimed at redrawing the map of Europe after Napoleon's fall. The victorious powers (Austria, Britain,

---

[1] Tulard, J. (2012). *Napoléon, chef de guerre*. Tallandier.
[2] Paul, W. (1976). *Kunstraub unter Napoleon*. Mann.

Prussia and Russia) attended these meetings, alongside the vanquished power (France), with Charles-Maurice de Talleyrand-Périgord representing Louis XVIII. The Final Act, embodying all the separate treaties, was signed on 9 June 1815 (nine days before the Battle of Waterloo). It led to around four decades of relative peace in Europe. Can as much be said of the Treaty of Versailles signed in 1919, the first drawn up in two languages, French and English? France hauled itself back on its feet after the Congress of Vienna. Can that be said of Germany after the Treaty of Versailles? Could it be that the Old World was better at negotiating and drafting treaties than our modern world?

In his book, *Europe's Last Summer: Who Started the Great War in 1914?*,[3] David Fromkin explains why it needs just one country to want war to precipitate a conflict. The American historian shows how German generals, seeing war as inevitable, manipulated events to precipitate a conflict waged on their own terms. Victorious, France resolved to make the Deutsches Reich pay for this disaster, which had put an end to European supremacy. It sought to destroy its neighbour economically so that it would not have the means to start a new war.

Into the Treaty of Versailles that ended the Great War was integrated the Covenant of the League of Nations. Some forty countries signed or were invited to accede to the Covenant, not however yesterday's enemy. The victors even refused to grant Germany's peace delegation the right to participate in the peace conference. Everything having been imposed on Germany, it was not a treaty but a diktat.

In Vienna, one diplomat was overheard saying, *"Le congrès ne marche pas, mais il danse!"*[4] Vanquished in the conflict, France welcomed the victors to its table, literally, for feasts worthy of its minister, Talleyrand, and its culinary history. The refrain at Versailles was, *"L'Allemagne paiera,"*[5] first uttered by Louis-Lucien Klotz, the French Finance Minister, before being repeated by Georges Clemenceau himself. Besides being stripped of large swaths of territory, Germany was required to pay a sum in gold that was more than double the total amount of gold mined since the discovery of America, i.e. the equivalent of 1,420 billion euros. Germany, bled dry after the Great War, thus became the most indebted country in the world.

---

[3] Fromkin, D. (2005) *Europe's Last Summer: Who Started the Great War in 1914?* Vintage.
[4] Congress isn't working, it is dancing!
[5] Germany shall pay.

It was a great power humiliated, driven into a corner, unable to find a peaceful economic way out. It felt hounded on all sides.

Less than two months after the armistice, the far-right party that would bring Hitler to power was formed. This party rejected from the outset the creation of the Weimar Republic, guilty in its eyes of having signed the Versailles treaty. In 1921, Matthias Erzberger, who signed the armistice as the head of the German delegation, was assassinated by an ultra-nationalist death squad. In January 1923, France and Belgium invaded and occupied the Ruhr in response to Germany defaulting on reparation payments. The invasion served as a pretext for the first putsch by the Nationalsozialistische Deutsche Arbeiterpartei later that year. The Beer Hall Putsch, as it became known, involved Hitler, Göring, Himmler and Ludendorff, who served as First Quartermaster-General of the Imperial Army's Great General Staff, the most senior officer below the Army's Chief of Staff, during the war. It failed. Six years later came the New York Stock Exchange crash on 24 October 1929, which would ultimately lead to the United States repatriating all funds held abroad. By February 1932, one-third of the German population was out of work. The Great Depression was the final straw, propelling Germany into a downward spiral in which the discourse of the far right thrived on the despair and poverty of the population, allowing Hitler to come to power through the ballot box. The rest is history.

As if a nod to a treaty negotiated without the intention of annihilating the vanquished, the Marshall Plan "against hunger, poverty, desperation and chaos"[6] was steered from 1949 onwards from the Hôtel Saint-Florentin on Place de la Concorde, the very place where Talleyrand lived, dined, entertained and ultimately died. The building now belongs to the United States but, much to its disappointment, visitors continue to come and see Talleyrand's home and not the place where the Marshall Plan was implemented. Despite the Marshall Plan, it would be an illusion to assume that the peace that followed the Second World War was better negotiated simply because a long period of peace ensued. The price of that peace was high, and we are still paying it: the Russians did not liberate Europe, but occupied half of it for more than four decades, oppressing farmers,

---

[6]Marshall, G. C., speech given to Harvard University on 5 June 1947. Officially, the Economic Recovery Act of 1948, but it became known as the Marshall Plan, named after US Secretary of State George Marshall.

lawyers, doctors, intellectuals and entrepreneurs whose wish was to live in a democracy and a free economy. Thirty years after the euphoria surrounding the fall of the Berlin Wall, it is becoming clear that the construction of the European Union will still take time before it can become, if member states really want it to be, the world's leading power.

Chapter 7

After the Great Recession, a Global Revolt Against the Established Order

France and the disenchantment of the French electorate

Over the last few decades, each global shock has strengthened international cooperation, often with the impetus coming from France. The first meeting of the G7 (France, Germany, Italy, Japan, the United Kingdom and the United States, with Canada joining two years later) was held in Rambouillet in 1975, at the invitation of Valéry Giscard d'Estaing, to respond to the oil crisis. The G20 was set up in response to the global financial crisis, again under the aegis of France. The G20 came into being when France had the rotating presidency of the European Council in the second half of 2008, when the financial crisis broke out. On 25 September 2008, Nicolas Sarkozy gave a speech in Toulon as President of both the French Republic and the European Council. This masterly, some would say masterful, speech deserves to be analysed for it encapsulates all necessary elements for exiting a major crisis.

The first part was addressed to the people of Europe and was cited, commented on and saluted by the entire European press. In it, President Sarkozy defined the framework for European action in dealing with the financial crisis, which would lead a few years later to the creation of the Banking Union. This Banking Union was a huge step forward for the European taxpayer. Such as envisaged, it had three pillars: the Single Supervisory Mechanism (SSM), the Single Resolution Mechanism (SRM) and the European Deposit Insurance Scheme (EDIS). Under the Single Supervisory Mechanism, the European Central Bank directly supervises the largest euro area banks, while the Single Resolution Mechanism is intended to ensure that, if a bank fails, there will be an orderly restructuring at a minimal cost for taxpayers and without harm to the real economy. These two mechanisms have the stated objective of severing the excessively close links between an individual member state and banks headquartered in the country. In everyday language, reference is often made to a "country and its banks". One might say that the moral hazard begins with this semantic shift.

Nicolas Sarkozy's great merit lies in the fact that, at the very start of the crisis, at the height of the financial meltdown, he mapped out the road ahead and what had to be done. His undeniable merit is that he did not make the wrong diagnosis. He understood from the outset that this was a deficiency in the global financial system that could be corrected by regulation, and that this financial crisis did not signal a failure as such of the market economy and global trade.

In his opening remarks, President Sarkozy said the main threat to the economy was fear, and it could only be overcome by telling the truth, thereby restoring confidence, without which there would be no resolution. There was no attempt to minimise the scope of the crisis. Rather, the emphasis was that the consequences would be serious and that the crisis risked derailing globalisation, intended he said to reduce social inequalities and avoid armed conflicts. He explained that if globalisation had not produced all the expected outcomes, it was because it had not relied sufficiently on the real economy, but on financial capitalism, involving the frenetic pursuit of ever-higher short-term returns, leading to reckless risk-taking. He went on to fustigate the inadequate regulation that allowed speculation to take root at the heart of the system. Work, he said, had not been given its rightful place in the real economy. He insisted that the crisis had not called capitalism into question, but a financial system that had become amoral and betrayed the values of the market economy. In his speech, he contrasted the effort of the worker with the easy money of speculation, the risk taken by the entrepreneur with the anonymity of the financial markets and productive capital with short-term capitalism. Finally, he insisted on the need for the country's economic transformation to be shaped by an industrial policy.

As France's President and the President-in-Office of the European Council, Nicolas Sarkozy pledged to "tighten up regulation of the banks to regulate the system, because banks are at the heart of the system."[1] He stressed that "self-regulation for everything was over" and how profoundly unjust it was for the taxpayer to pay for the banks' losses. A decade after the financial crisis and the Toulon speech, the Banking Union is up and running. The only criticism is that it needs to be strengthened and that speed is of the essence.

Nicolas Sarkozy also stressed the need to control credit rating agencies, for they were found wanting in their rating of the famous subprime vehicles. The European Securities and Markets Authority (ESMA) was established as early as 1 January 2011. As part of its mandate to ensure effective and efficient supervision of financial markets, it is the single direct supervisor of credit rating agencies registered in the European Union.

In Toulon, looking beyond the confines of France and the European Union, Nicolas Sarkozy insisted on the need for a global response to the international financial crisis. He stressed that the way out of the crisis could not be at the expense of certain countries, but that it required a coordinated response that would demand efforts by each and every one. On 12 October 2008, the first ever meeting of euro area heads of state or governments took place at the Élysée Palace, hosted by Nicolas Sarkozy. It was at this summit that the European bank rescue plan was adopted. It would then serve as a model for the United States. Accompanied by José Manuel Durão Barroso, the President of the European Commission, Nicolas Sarkozy travelled to Camp David to convince President Bush of the need for a global response to the financial crisis. In his political memoir, *La France pour la vie*, the French President explained that "Since the crisis originated in the United States, it was impossible to do it without them. So I decided to convince the President of the United States, George Bush, to take the initiative in the counter-offensive."[2] He describes his meeting with George Bush as follows: "I wanted to convince him that we needed to bring together in Washington, as a matter of urgency, the representatives of the world's largest economies to try to coordinate their economic policies, influence the course of events and begin to regulate world

---

[1] www.lemonde.fr/politique/article/2008/09/25/le-discours-de-nicolas-sarkozy-a-toulon_1099795_823448.html#W5UmpzbWf5PPGxTe.99.

[2] Sarkozy, N. (2006) *La France pour la vie*. Plon.

finance, which was in great need of it. George Bush was initially reluctant. [...] His abiding fear was that he would be put in the dock. [...] And so was born the G20, which has managed the world's major economic issues since 2008."[3]

In his keynote speech in Toulon, Nicolas Sarkozy went even further, talking about the currency wars that were harming trade exchanges and also consumers by reducing the benefits they had a right to expect from globalisation. He talked about the need to create the tools for a global regulatory framework to ensure that globalisation would be inclusive. His aim was to ensure that regulations inherited from the 20th century were fit for the realities and challenges of the 21st century, so that each citizen in each country might benefit.

In the second part of his speech, he addressed the French people. Once again, he was at pains to restore confidence by asserting that the state would guarantee the bank deposits of customers and take the necessary measures to ensure the continued financing of productive investment. This is legally inaccurate but politically crucial, a matter of getting across a vital message though it meant taking some liberties with the legal technicalities. Put it down to a great politician having taken to the stage, not a technocrat. To facilitate real estate investments, he announced a law in favour of housing. To better withstand the crisis, he recalled all the measures taken to boost purchasing power, and an increase in the research tax credit to 30% to support innovation-based growth.

To ensure that the crisis did not exacerbate social inequalities and, consequently, generate a political risk, as the 1929 crisis had, Nicolas Sarkozy decided to create the *"revenu de solidarité active"* (RSA), a new social security benefit guaranteeing a minimum income to the working poor and unemployed, financed by a tax on financial income. He also increased the minimum old-age allowance and the most modest survivors' pensions and granted a bonus to those in receipt of minimum social benefits. It was all about restoring confidence, which was essential if France was to withstand the worst crisis since the Second World War. This approach made economic sense, since it would inject money into the real economy through household consumption. It was also politically visionary, because political extremism always feeds on the fear of social downgrading and poverty. The risk was that history could repeat itself as it did after the Great Depression.

---

[3] *Ibid.*

Finally, addressing future generations, Nicolas Sarkozy called for sustainable growth, pledging to implement the recommendations of the so-called Grenelle de l'environnement, an open multi-party debate held the previous year to define public policy on environmental and sustainable development.

Unquestionably, the Toulon speech helped to restore confidence and contain the short-term political risk. In the presidential election that followed, the far-right leader Marine Le Pen won just 18% of the vote in the first round, failing to qualify for the second round. At the other extreme of the political spectrum, Jean-Luc Mélenchon got just 11% of the vote.[4]

The far-right and far-left parties did, however, go on to staggering gains by the time of the next presidential election in 2017. In the first round, Marine Le Pen obtained 21.30% and Jean-Luc Mélenchon 19.58% of the vote.[5]

The disenchantment of the French electorate is reflected in the abstention rate, which rose to 25.4% in the second round of the 2017 presidential election, up six percentage points compared with the previous election. Emmanuel Macron got 66% of the vote to Marine Le Pen's 34%.

This is in stark contrast to the 2002 election, when the far-right candidate qualified for the second round. For one thing, the abstention rate was lower at only 20.3%. More importantly, Jacques Chirac won by a landslide, getting 82% of the vote to Jean-Marie Le Pen's 18%.

It is clear that, over the medium term, the Great Recession did change the political landscape. Emmanuel Macron triumphed in the live debate held between the two rounds, brushing off Marine Le Pen, who appeared distracted at times. Even so, the far-right candidate got two times more votes than her father in 2012.

In other countries, the outcome of the Brexit referendum and the election of Donald Trump are further examples of the effect of the Great Recession on the rise of nationalist extremism.

International economic cooperation had held up well since the Second World War, but in the decade or so that followed the crisis, it was rattled by the political context. The British vote to leave the European Union and the election of Donald Trump as President of the United States have

---

[4] www.interieur.gouv.fr/Elections/Les-resultats/Presidentielles/elecresult__PR2012/(path)/PR2012/FE.html.

[5] www.interieur.gouv.fr/Elections/Les-resultats/Presidentielles/elecresult__presidentielle-2017/(path)/presidentielle-2017/FE.html.

undermined the international liberal economic order built up by these two countries after the defeat of Nazism, and which went on to be strengthened by the fall of the Berlin Wall.

Having brought down the two great totalitarian regimes of the 20th century, the builders of multilateralism seem to have become its demolishers. Will Joe Biden's election contribute to a return to the multilateralism of the pre-Trump era, or will the focus be exclusively on holding back China's economic development? Will the United States regain leadership of the globalised world? Or will this role fall to the European Union or even China? Will a hegemony other than a Western hegemony be accepted by the world when not ruined by a world war? Or will it have been shaken to such an extent by the COVID-19 pandemic, and then by a war between two European states, that it will accept Chinese hegemony?

In the century marked by the advent of big data and digitalisation, economic coordination could be more effective than ever. It could benefit all the world's citizens if it strengthens the fight against terrorism, supports environmental protection and promotes international trade in a way such that the benefits are fairly distributed.

The United States that voted Trump

Though the United States was at the origin of the 2008 crisis, it emerged stronger economically, but weaker as a nation. The risk of political and social frailty, one of the main components of political risk, has increased significantly since the subprime crisis, to the point of electing Donald Trump and bringing about a profound change in the structure of modern American politics. The exacerbation of inequalities in the wake of the 2008 crisis was largely responsible for all this.

Poverty is not measured in the same way from one country to another. The general rule is that people are classified as poor when their equalised disposable household income is between 50% and 60% below the median prevailing in the country. However, since the 1960s, the United States has set thresholds of around $12,000, $16,000, $20,000 and $24,000 for one-person, two-person, three-person and four-person households, respectively. By way of comparison, the European poverty line for one person is set at around $19,200.[6]

---

[6] www.lisdatacenter.org/our-data/.

According to the US Census Bureau, the official poverty rate in the United States reached 12.7% in 2016,[7] having increased slightly from 12.5% in 2007, which was the year that preceded the crisis. This means that 40.6 million Americans were living in poverty in 2016, bringing the spotlight to bear on the inequality that lies behind the American dream.

In the United States, though women surpass men in terms of educational attainment (i.e. bachelor's degree or higher), they were harder hit by the crisis than men in terms of their income. In 2016, the median income of full-time, year-round workers averaged $51,640 for men and $41,554 for women.[8] This was the first time since 2007 that the wage gap between men and women had not widened, but closed slightly. What is striking is that gender differences in poverty rates were more pronounced for those aged 18–64. In 2016, the poverty rate for women aged 18–64 was 13.4%, while the poverty rate for men in this age group was 9.7%. The poverty rate for women aged 65 and older, so having retired, was 10.6%, while the poverty rate for men in this age group was 7.6%. For children under age 18, the poverty rate for girls was 18.4%, while the poverty rate for boys was 17.6%.[9] One immediate consequence of the wage discrimination experienced by women is that children, who more often than not are cared for by their mother rather than their father in the case of a one-person household, are the category most affected by poverty.

In 2016, the poverty rate for children under age 18 in both male- and female-householder families reached 18.0%, when poverty rates were 11.6% for people aged 18–64 and 9.3% for people aged 65 and older. The number in children under 18 in poverty was 13.3 million. The poverty rate was 38% for Black children and 30% for Hispanic children. About half or more precisely 49.1% of related children under age 6 in families with a female householder were in poverty in 2016. With wealth concentrated in the hands of 1% of the population, and a reduction in the tax burden for the wealthiest, less was invested in child education and protection. In the United States, access to healthcare and education for a child depends more on the parents' income than in other developed countries.

In the 21st century, the best way out of poverty is through higher education. In the United States, only 4.5% of people with at least three years

---

[7] www.census.gov/library/publications/2017/demo/p60-259.html.
[8] *Ibid.*
[9] *Ibid.*

of higher education (i.e. bachelor's degree or higher) were in poverty in 2016.

In 1980, university tuition fees were around $9,000 dollars on average, compared with which median household income was $46,000. In 2016, fees have since increased to $22,000 on average, compared with which median household income increased to $59,000. Obviously, the increase in tuition fees varied from one state to another. Between the 2007–2008 and 2012–2013 academic years, tuition fees rose by more than 70% at California's public universities. In fact, the state of California spends more on its prison system than on universities. On average, tuition fees increased by 27% after the crisis, partly because of cuts in public aids. Tuition fees are often funded by loans taken out by students. The student loan debt crisis worsened in the wake of the 2008 crisis, as young graduates struggled to find jobs and those who did were paid less than before the financial crisis. It was only in 2015 that median household income began to rise. In 2016, it increased by 3.2% from the 2015 median. The ballooning of student loans held back consumption and delayed the recovery of the residential real estate market, which was at the origin of the subprime crisis.

The difficulties of young people getting started in life are reflected in the fact that young American adults are living with their parents for longer and longer. Yet, the United States is not a country of "stay-at-homes": young Americans dream of economic independence from the age of 16, typically the minimum age to obtain a restricted driver's licence. In 2007, there were 19.7 million shared households (that include at least one additional adult, a person aged 18 or older, who is not the householder, spouse or cohabiting partner of the householder). In 2017, this number had increased to 24.6 million.

In 2017, an estimated 28% or 12.4 million adults aged 25–34 were additional adults in someone else's household. It is estimated that 16.1% or 7.1 million lived with their parents. Adults aged 25–34 living with their parents in 2017 had an official 2016 poverty rate of 7.3%.

The American dream attracts many immigrants. But, are they able to make a living in the United States? In 2016, the number in poverty for the native-born population reached 34 million. Among the foreign-born population, 15.1% or 6.6 million were in poverty. Of these 6.6 million, 4.6 million were not yet American citizens.

In an opinion piece published by the New York Times on 14 April 2013, Joseph Stiglitz, the winner of the 2011 Nobel Prize in Economic Sciences, blamed these inequalities on "a tax system stacked against the 99%," the wealthiest 1% of Americans owning about 40% of the nation's wealth. He wrote, "Put simply, the very rich don't pay their fair share. The richest 400 individual taxpayers, with an average income of more than $200 million, pay less than 20% of their income in taxes — far lower than mere million-aires, who pay about 25% of their income in taxes, and about the same as those earning a mere $200,000 to $500,000. And in 2009, 116 of the top 400 earners — almost a third — paid less than 15% of their income in taxes."[10] Joseph Stiglitz made the point that the top marginal income tax rate remained at 70% through the 1960s and 1970s, but was 39.6% in 2013. The low effective tax rate introduced in the 1980s explains why the rich got far richer. Since 2013, inequalities have been exacerbated.

The real income of most Americans is lower than it was in 1997, which shows that the trickle-down theory has not worked. The rich are getting even richer, without this lifting the poor out of poverty. Even the International Monetary Fund (IMF) has acknowledged for several years that it is not possible to achieve growth and stability without addressing income inequality. The IMF states that, based on a study of economic history and an analysis of available data, there is no compelling evidence to suggest that a redistribution of a country's wealth can be detrimental to achieving sustained growth. The macroeconomic data available to the IMF indicates that there is no trade-off between economic growth and redistribution through an efficient tax system. Scandinavian countries have long understood this economic truth. Their democracies are not under threat, but those of countries that pit economic growth against redistribution are.

The Patriotic Millionaires is a group of several hundred high-net-worth Americans, including Warren Buffett, lobbying for a redistributive tax system and a "liveable" wage. Their credo in the words of Ron Garret, one of its members, is "Millionaires are not the cause of a robust economy, they are the result of a robust economy." Concerning Trump's tax reform in favour of the rich, millionaire Robert Goldschmidt stated, "Make no mistake, the trillion-dollar tax cuts for the wealthy proposed by Trump and his friends in Congress will create deficit dollars. Sooner or later those deficit dollars will be repaid by cutting 'entitlements', i.e. taking from working families and the poor." That is what happened, unfortunately, for the most modest American households.

---

[10] https://archive.nytimes.com/opinionator.blogs.nytimes.com/2013/04/14/a-tax-system-stacked-against-the-99-percent/.

Yet, Donald Trump was brought to power by the fear of social demotion and poverty.

Exit poll data for the 2016 presidential election was collected by the National Election Pool, a consortium of American news organisations (ABC News, Associated Press, CBS News, CNN, Fox News, and NBC News).[11] According to exit polling information, electors who voted for Donald Trump had the following profile:

- Mainly white men (white women voted in majority for Hillary Clinton) aged 45 and over, married, and having served in the US military;
- 67% of whites who voted for Donald Trump had not studied beyond high school;
- Had income of between $50,000 and $99,999;
- Lived in a suburban area; and
- 90% were Republicans.

The exit poll data clearly shows that it was the middle class (fearful of social demotion and poverty) that elected Donald Trump. He won 46% of the popular vote, but more electoral votes than his rival Hillary Clinton, who won 48% of the popular vote — the rest going to the other minor candidates. But, Donald Trump's score reached 50% among Americans earning between $50,000 and $99,999, and his score was weaker among more affluent voters.

A sign of this sentiment of social demotion, 79% of Donald Trump's voters considered that the condition of the national economy was poor and 77% that their financial situation was worse currently compared to four years before. 63% of these voters considered that life for the next generation of Americans would be worse than currently.

As to what had caused their social demotion, 65% considered that international trade had taken away US jobs. 83% wanted illegal immigrants to be deported immediately to their home country. 86% supported Trump's plan to build a US wall along the entire Mexican border.

It is interesting to note that when a country experiences a major crisis, rather than becoming aware of misguided policy decisions, the finger is often pointed at an enemy from without. International trade and globalisation are frequently singled out, even though there is economic evidence

---

[11] www.nytimes.com/interactive/2016/11/08/us/politics/electionexit-polls.html.

that international trade has always strengthened prosperity and promoted peace.

The United Kingdom that voted for Brexit

The United Kingdom has seen much the same evolution in inequality as the United States. In its report *Living standards, poverty and inequality in the UK: 2017*,[12] the British Institute for Fiscal Studies (IFS) explains that, after falling slightly during the 1960s and 1970s, inequality between the top 1% of the income distribution and the rest started to increase in the 1980s. It continued to rise up until the onset of the Great Recession, which exacerbated income inequality. Overall, the top 1%'s income share more than doubled from 3.4% in 1980 to 8.7% in 2009–2010.

Although the number of people in work has risen, earnings growth has been so weak that employment income in the UK in 2015–2016 was still lower than that prior to the recession. Household income data for 2015–2016 shows that the median income is only 3.7% above the level in 2007–2008.

In the United Kingdom also, it is the young and children that have paid the price of the crisis. In 2015–2016, median income for those aged 60 and over was 10% higher than it was in 2007–2008, but for adults aged 22–30 it was 4% lower. According to the IFS, these differences are primarily due to the negative labour market impacts of the recession, which were far more pronounced among younger people. Real earnings for this group were still 12% lower in 2015–2016 than before the recession. In other words, the gap in the standard of living of seniors and younger people has widened.

In 2016, 10% of all British children lived in persistent poverty (defined as being in income poverty in three of the last four years), with this reaching 38% among children in households that have been workless for at least three of the last four years. Children have been the collateral victims of persistent worklessness and persistently low earnings, the data for households on the lowest income showing that very rarely did it increase in the case of lone-parent households and families with more than three children.

The poverty rate declined sharply over the decade that preceded the crisis. Between 1995–1996 and 2005–2006, the absolute poverty rate decreased by 17 percentage points. This decrease was largely driven by

---

[12] www.ifs.org.uk/publications/9539.

changes in welfare spending under the Labour government (which pursued a redistributive policy, specifically targeting children and pensioners in lower-income households) and by real earnings growth for those in work. The decade after the 2008 crisis was extremely disappointing in this respect, with the COVID-19 crisis leading to a deterioration of the situation.

The famous so-called zero-hours contract has become a symbol of these years, even though its legal framework dates from the late 1990s. Its main characteristic is that it does not guarantee a minimum number of hours of work in a given week. With this contract, employees become the adjustment variable for businesses. This is not unique to the United Kingdom: other countries such as New Zealand had also adopted it, but in 2016 the New Zealand Parliament unanimously passed a bill to ban this controversial practice. It is hard to imagine this ever happening in the United Kingdom: until the 2008 crisis, there were around 200 thousand contracts that did not guarantee a minimum number of hours, where work had actually been carried out under those contracts. With the crisis, this number has shot up: according to the Office for National Statistics, there were 1.4 million such contracts in May 2017.[13]

Zero-hours contracts apply to workers in both the public and private sectors. According to the Office for National Statistics, a worker on a zero-hours contract typically works 26 hours a week on average, but may not work at all if not called in by the employer, even when the worker would want to work. Workers are at the beck and call of their employer, with no guarantee of being given work.

According to the Office for National Statistics, 5% of UK workers were employed under zero-hours contracts in 2017. This contract was rarely a choice on the part of the worker, even though its flexibility could be considered advantageous by some students. In fact, 17.9% of workers on zero-hours contracts in 2017 were in full-time education. However, before contracts of this type flourished, many students were able to fund their studies by working under ordinary contracts.

What is the profile of people having reported that their main employment was under a zero-hours contract? The profile has not changed much since these contracts were introduced, these contracts still concerning mainly women and people at the youngest end of the age range. Women make up a bigger share, 57.7%, while 33.8% of people on these contracts

---

[13] www.ons.gov.uk/employmentandlabourmarket/peopleinwork/earningsandworkinghours/articles/contractsthatdonotguaranteeaminimumnumberofhours/september2017#summary.

are aged 16–24. Some 65.4% of people on these contracts worked part-time (compared with 25.4% of people employed under contracts other than a zero-hours contract). These are the social categories most affected by poverty.

It is very surprising to note that almost a quarter of employees on zero-hours contracts work in the health and social service industry. It is hard to imagine the quality of medical care not being affected from having recourse to this type of contract, with the implication this has in terms of staff turnover. Paradoxically, only 10.5% of workers on zero-hours contracts work in the accommodation and food industry, closely followed by transport and education.

It is also very surprising to find that 24% of businesses with 250 or more employees make some use of zero-hours contracts, compared with around 4% of businesses with fewer than ten employees. Yet, small businesses are less able to cushion a fall in demand. To their credit, these businesses have not made headcount the adjustment variable.

Like the election of Donald Trump in the United States, the 51.9% Leave vote in the Brexit referendum held on 23 June 2016 reflected the victory of populism fuelled by rising inequality and poverty, as well as a political discourse constantly blaming the European Union for these woes. This wave of populism swept across the Anglo-Saxon world as well as other European countries (France, Germany, Austria, Poland, Hungary and Greece). In these countries, when things are going well, politicians congratulate themselves; but, whenever things go wrong, they blame the faceless bureaucrats in Brussels.

Regrettably, the resources of the European Commission's Legal Service cannot be applied to bringing libel or slander actions against those defaming the European Union. In the case of the Brexit campaign, if the European Commission had responded to the accusations, the outcome might have been different. The political discourse, riddled with falsehoods, blaming the European Union for the rise in social inequalities, was undoubtedly a decisive factor in the Brexit Leave vote.

An analysis of the Brexit vote by YouGov[14] shows that the higher the household income, the smaller the proportion of Leave votes. There was 62% support for leaving the European Union among voters from households with income of less than £20,000 a year, declining to 53% for the £20,000–£40,000 bracket, then 42% for the £40,000–£60,000 bracket and

---

[14] yougov.co.uk/news/2016/06/27/how-britain-voted/.

only 35% among voters from households with income of more than £60,000 a year. Age was a major fault line. The desire of younger generations, more concerned about the long term than their elders, was clearly to remain in the European Union: 71% of Britons aged 18–24 and 54% of those aged 25–49 voted Remain.

For poor voters who felt forgotten by the economic, social and political system, the Leave vote was a way to express their discontent. The misguided belief was that their misfortune was due to immigration. Yet, before the 2008 financial crisis, wages grew despite the higher immigration. The increased mobility of people, and therefore immigrants, is seen as a major aspect of globalisation. Scapegoating immigrants was easier than blaming the failings of financial regulation, although this triggered the financial crisis. Yet, the fact is that European immigrants are generally younger, better educated and less likely to claim welfare benefits than native-born Britons. Reducing immigration can be expected to hurt public finances and will not necessarily help reduce inequalities.

The entire British population will suffer economically from the consequences of Brexit. The deterioration in the standard of living of the most vulnerable social groups will push them further into poverty. The post-Brexit decade is likely to be worse for the most precarious individuals than the post-subprime crisis decade.

Chapter 8

Will There Be a Global Change Post-COVID?

Pandemics recur on average every 25 years, with different health and socio-economic effects depending on their severity and the state of the world. There are many scenarios as to the consequences of the COVID-19 crisis.

On the one hand, pessimists like Michel Houellebecq believe that the post-pandemic world "will be the same, only a little worse."[1] Would "a little worse" stretch to a far-left or far-right party coming to power in France if there is an exponential rise in unemployment? No party, at the far left or far right, will campaign on a Frexit platform that might scare off pensioners. You don't win elections without this electorate, and the mere talk of a Frexit would put their nest eggs at risk. Once in power, it would be a different matter. In a context where the health and economic crisis leaves the French population poorer, who is to say which of the Leave or Remain vote would prevail if a far-left or far-right government were to hold a referendum?

On the other hand, optimists believe that the roaring twenties will follow the COVID-19 crisis in the 21st century, just as they did in the last after the Great Influenza pandemic (also known by the common misnomer of the Spanish flu) caused by the H1N1 influenza A virus. The optimists expect the 2020s will be just like the 1920s. In any case, this apparently

---

[1] www.francetvinfo.fr/sante/maladie/coronavirus/coronavirus-pourmichel-houellebecq-le-monde-d-apres-sera-le-meme-en-un-peupire_3948117.html.

seductive scenario warrants taking a closer look at the mythical Spanish flu pandemic.

The pandemic spread at the end of the First World War, in 1918 and 1919. According to the Institut Pasteur,[2] it may also have originated in China, and more specifically in the Guangzhou or Canton region, where it may have contaminated a US battalion before its return to Boston. The first documented case was at Fort Riley, a military establishment in Kansas. By then, the virus had already mutated, becoming more virulent. It was this variant that was introduced in Europe with the arrival of American troops. The circulation of the virus was facilitated by the war. COVID-19 was spread by trade exchanges in a globalised economy. To this day, the reason for the extreme virulence of the 1918 pandemic has not been explained scientifically. That is despite a complete genomic sequence of the virus in 2005, thanks to viral RNA isolated from the lungs of an Inuit woman who likely died due to complications from the 1918 virus and was exhumed from the permafrost in Alaska by Swedish pathologist Johan Hultin.

The pandemic was soon misnamed the "Spanish flu" simply because Spanish newspapers were among the first to report its effects. Spain being a neutral country in the conflict was not bound by wartime censorship. The censorship was so effective in belligerent nations that there was a total blackout. Moreover, it was easier to keep a tally of the loss of life due to this virus in a country that had not been bled dry by the Great War. The deaths were not attributable to a war-weary population, and the counting was not left to the military. In Spain, the flu killed around 150,000 people, or 7.1 per 1,000 population.

Having struck at much the same time as the Allied victory over Germany in 1918, and given that "the press had orders not to talk about the epidemic so as not to panic civilians and demoralise the troops,"[3] the Spanish flu remained less vivid in the collective memory in France than in Spain. Nevertheless, at the time, French newspapers were full of obituaries and advertisements for products designed to treat the "Spanish flu", recommending people to take aspirin (*"La Grippe espagnole se traite par*

---

[2] Hannoun, C. (1993) *La Grippe*, Documents de la Conférence de l'Institut Pasteur. La Grippe Espagnole de 1918. Ed Techniques Encyclopédie Médico-Chirurgicale (EMC), Maladies infectieuses. Vol. 8-069-A-10.

[3] www.biusante.parisdescartes.fr/sfhm/hsm/HSMx2004x038x002/HSMx2004x038x 002x0165.pdf.

l'Aspirine Usines du Rhône") or add an antiseptic product when doing their laundry (*"Pour éviter la grippe, les autorités médicales recommandent de faire bouillir et laver le linge en employant la Boréale, produit antiseptique qui détruit les germes de la contagion"*).[4]

It is estimated that the Great Influenza pandemic killed more than 40 million people in the world (twice as many as the Great War, which has made a far more indelible impression in France). There were 400,000 deaths in France,[5] the epidemic claiming the lives of poet and dramatist Edmond Rostand, who died at the age of 50, three days after catching the flu at the theatre, and of poet Guillaume Apollinaire, who was 38. In contrast to COVID-19, the Great Influenza affected the young and spared the old (i.e. over 60, who admittedly were far fewer in number in those days). For example, in Bordeaux, 14% of those who died from the Great Influenza were less than 20 years old, 56% were 20–40 years old, 22% were 40–60 years old and 8% were more than 60 years old.[6]

In her doctoral thesis submitted in 1919, Marguerite Barbier, a Paris hospital intern, explained, "Healthy, vigorous patients with no previous pathological conditions succumbed within a few days, whereas flu sufferers aged between 50 and 70, some of whom were poor wrecks from devastated regions (by the war), made a quick and total recovery."[7]

To "stimulate" patients in Paris hospitals, they were administered rum, this being a national tipple, in the search for a miracle cure, reminiscent of the rise and fall of chloroquine/hydroxychloroquine, this drug repurposing not living up to the early media hype.

According to the Institut Pasteur, the 1918 A (H1N1) virus remained in circulation until 1957.[8] Other viruses derived from the 1918 virus also circulated among the population for an even lengthier period. Many people having been exposed, to a greater or lesser extent, to other H1N1 viruses, this induced a degree of immunity that provided some protection against the 2009 H1N1 virus. This last virus is still in circulation, but it has become seasonal in nature, and one of its strains is now used in the composition of the annual flu vaccine.

---

[4] www.historim.fr/2020/03/la-grippe-espagnole-1918-1920-issy-les.html.

[5] https://www.pasteur.fr/en/research-journal/reports/keeping-close-eye-influenza.

[6] Guillaume, P. (1978) *La grippe à Bordeaux en 1918*, Ann. démo. hist., pp. 167–173.

[7] Barbier, M. (1919) *La Grippe de 1918–1919, Thèse pour le doctorat en médecine.* Paris. https://exhibits.lib.unc.edu/items/show/5785.

[8] https://www.pasteur.fr/en/research-journal/reports/keeping-close-eye-influenza.

Over the same timeframe, the Spanish flu pandemic was far deadlier than the COVID-19 pandemic. However, it was followed by a period of very strong economic expansion and a cultural renaissance, as borne out by the sumptuous art deco buildings erected across Europe in the 1920s.[9]

Will there be the same economic growth after the COVID-19 crisis as between 1920 and 1929, or will the economy plunge straight into a crisis like that of 1929? This certainly merits being examined from both an economic and a social perspective.

In France, gross domestic product (GDP), an aggregate measuring the strength of the economy, fell by 8.3% in 2020,[10] compared with which there was a decline of just 2.6% during the 2009 global financial crisis.

In 2020, because the French state supported the economy through state-guaranteed loans, sector-specific measures and emergency measures, there were fewer corporate bankruptcies than at the start of the 2008 crisis. In fact, the number of corporate bankruptcies decreased by 39% year on year in 2020 according to the Banque de France.[11] This decrease was observed in all sectors of activities and for most categories of enterprises. The central bank explained that "This decrease [...] results: firstly, from the temporary impact of the lockdown on the operation of commercial jurisdictions and regulatory changes that temporarily modified the dates for characterizing and declaring a firm as insolvent; secondly, from all support measures that provide cash-flow assistance or enable firms to reduce or delay the payment of certain charges, and thus the risk of defaulting on these payments (partial activity scheme, state-guaranteed loans, solidarity fund, moratoria, etc.)."[12]

The risk of corporate defaults is bound to increase when the state scales back its intervention. A wave of restructurings and redundancies is likely to ensue. Rising unemployment will push the poorest workers deeper into poverty and sap the middle class. To limit the attendant political and social risk, the state should withdraw its aid gradually rather than stop it abruptly.

During the economic recovery, there will need to be trade-offs, ending support for non-performing businesses and allocating resources in favour of

---

[9]The International Exhibition of Modern Decorative and Industrial Arts held in Paris in 1925 marked the apogee of the Art Deco style to which it gave its name.

[10]www.insee.fr/fr/statistiques/5018361.

[11]https://www.banque-france.fr/sites/default/files/webstat_pdf/def_ent_2233_fr_si_defaillances_202101_fr.pdf.

[12]*Ibid.*

productive businesses, targeting innovative and fast-growing undertakings, notably in the technology, health and energy transition sectors. Innovation means staying ahead in the global economic race to generate the financial resources needed to fund the current social security system over the long term. To paraphrase Talleyrand, the most important thing is not to spend little, but to earn a lot. That is achieved through innovation, as this leads to comfortable margins. The strength of the economic recovery as well as the timeframe will therefore depend on the ability to select the economic sectors to be supported. They need to be those that will drive economic growth and performances, not those that, because in decline or facing cut-throat competition at the country level, will consume public resources in vain. All nations having experienced periods of strong growth (Asian countries in recent decades) have followed this common-sense principle.

The major crisis experienced in 2020 was also when society really switched to digital applications. During the first lockdown, we learned to live in a virtual world that was more vibrant than the real world. From an economic point of view, the recovery is therefore likely to be K-shaped: businesses that are well positioned in this digital society will experience exponential growth, the others vertiginous falls. This is borne out by the evolution in the market capitalisation of the GAFA (Google, Amazon, Facebook and Amazon). All these Big Techs outperformed the market in 2020. The market capitalisation of Apple, another Big Tech, exceeds that of the 40 companies in the CAC index. At the global level, the market capitalisation of the 20 leading technology companies analysed by Fabernovel[13] — including GAFA plus Microsoft (GAFAM) and their Chinese counterparts, Baidu, Alibaba, Tencent and Xiaomi (BATX) — recorded a median increase of 71% in 2020 compared with 2019. In the years preceding the COVID-19 crisis, their market capitalisation increased by 31% a year on average. After the COVID-19 crisis, the energy and financial sectors are bound to perk up as the economic recovery gets into gear. They will probably remain the top two sectors based on market capitalisation, but to be sure the technology sector will claim third place. The size effect will continue to play more and more in favour of now increasingly irreplaceable technology companies, which are well aware that they are major financial powerhouses and society influencers.

This digital acceleration will also have a considerable impact in social terms. Beyond their financial clout, the impact of social networks has

---

[13] www.fabernovel.com/fr/clients/studies/gafanomics-quarterly-q4-2020.

been clear to see: they are an effective counterweight to the excesses of certain public figures, political or otherwise, but they are also accelerators of fake news and vectors of radicalisation. Like the spoken language they tend to replace, chats and posts can be the worst or the best of things. Their impact on people's behaviour is increasingly sensitive and, naturally, will have an indirect economic impact as a result.

For millions of French people, the lockdowns meant switching to remote working, which became an integral part of everyday life. While for some, it was a dream come true, others dreaded it, but almost everyone got to try it out. Between those who lived through the first lockdown with their window looking onto the trees of their second home or beside their swimming pool, and those sharing a tiny apartment, intended for eating and sleeping, with children forced to stay at home, the experiences were different. But, what they all have in common is the attention now given to housing conditions. If you can be locked down in your own home by the authorities, you might as well be comfortable there. And, since you can now work part of the time from home, you might as well think big. At the same time, many employees and civil servants do not see there being quite so many benefits to living close to their employer, typically in the city centre. There will undoubtedly be a move away from large urban centres, which are expensive and therefore synonymous with small surface areas, towards greener, more distant but more affordable areas. This will affect the whole ecosystem linked to the main home: shops, schools, public services, etc.

Another sociological factor brought on by COVID-19 was the mistrust of the "other". Symbolised by the famous social distancing, this mistrust is the direct consequence of the fear of being infected by a carrier who, very often, is asymptomatic and therefore unaware of his dangerousness. People had to stay at safe distances, wear masks and use hand sanitizers — in short, avoid physical contact. Obviously, it is easier to keep your distance from strangers, about whom very little is known and who are the sum of all fears, than from your own family. That was why the authorities discouraged family gatherings, even for Christmas. In many countries, the residents of retirement homes were quarantined without any medical care, leaving those seriously ill to die without seeing their loved ones again, while condemning all the others to a slow death from being cut off from their loved ones. Where the social bond was weakened, it can be restored once the virus is under control and everyone is reassured and convinced that there is a visible improvement in the situation. The family bond, on the other hand, will be more difficult to re-establish, with so many emotions having been stirred up. What was witnessed might be called intergenerational egoism, in reference to the treatment of the old at the end of their life, on the one hand, and of the young, notably the students, about to take their full place, on the other hand. Old and young were told to isolate from the world so that the laborious generations might "put in an extra shift". What will undoubtedly remain is a rather altered vision, for many, of how old age is going to be organised. And, for younger people, there will be some disenchantment about the real priority given to education.

Will the 2020s see as many technological breakthroughs as the 1920s? The 1920s were characterised by revolutionary inventions that added to the general euphoria of those who survived the Great War and Great Influenza. In the medical field, for example, the first adhesive bandages appeared, as did the vaccine against tuberculosis (discovered by Albert Calmette and Camille Guérin), as well as insulin and penicillin, the pacemaker and the electroencephalogram. The start of the 2020s is also promising in this field, with the development of messenger RNA vaccines[14] against COVID-19. This technology could also be used to combat other diseases (such as AIDS). A Phase I clinical trial testing a novel vaccine approach to prevent HIV was completed in February 2021 in the United States. The scene would appear to be set for some major medical discoveries. Equalling the 1920s will be quite a challenge, however.

Many of the creature comforts we enjoy were developed in the 1920s: refrigerators, gramophones, telephones, radios, hairdryers, electric shavers, televisions, remote controls, photocopiers, light-emitting diodes, air conditioners, PVC and fibreglass, quartz and electric clocks, etc. This was the decade when the aeroplane became a means of transport. Steam engines were replaced by diesel engines, and the invention of the injection pump made these engines more efficient. Some of the world's wealthiest families were behind these innovations. Fortunes were not made in the service sector, as is the case nowadays, but in the industrial sector. Will the industrial discoveries of the 2020s match those of the 1920s? If fossil and nuclear energies were replaced by new energies to achieve carbon neutrality by 2050, that would be so, and the planet would be saved from the most worrying threat of all: global warming.

---

[14] www.inserm.fr/information-en-sante/c-est-quoi/secret-fabrication-c-est-quoi-arn-messager.

The fact remains that companies will emerge from the COVID-19 crisis laden with debt. In most cases, governments have done their utmost to support them and are hardly in a stronger position than they are, save for those countries, such as Germany, that have been very prudently managed for decades. Allowing the accelerated bankruptcies of zombie companies could weaken the most exposed banks, reducing their ability to extend credits and finance the recovery.

So, here we are again, considering the role of the banks, no longer as the cause but as a way out of the crisis.

Part III

Banks: Mirror of Our Society?

In God We Trust[*]

"In God We Trust" appears on all US banknotes. No one is saying which singular God we are talking about, but it is clear that the greenback is not a pious image. It is the materialisation of a currency that has become the currency of international trade. It has been used for smuggling in the most unlikely of places, as well as in furtherance of US policy, for the Marshall Plan after the Second World War and now for Joe Biden's Build Back Better Plan. The dollar has become to money what English is to language — the universal reference.

From time immemorial, some people have worshipped money much as others have worshipped power or music. In many rich countries, gradual disaffection with true religion has been accompanied by a growing materialism that has led to a sometimes unbridled quest for wealth. The greenback may well have become a kind of God for many men and women: we respect it, turning to it like a saviour when things go wrong, fighting and sometimes killing for it. We may even sacrifice to it what we hold most dear — our health, our friends, our principles.

---

[*]The motto of the United States, inscribed on its coins and notes.

And yet, it is just another banknote like all the others issued around the world, originally by commercial banks and now increasingly by central banks. To understand the power of these banks, which may no longer print large quantities of banknotes, but do create money in the course of their business, let's take a closer look.

Chapter 9

The Profession's Metamorphosis

The oldest profession in the world

Many professions claim to be the oldest in the world. Banking is one of them. Trade between people has developed ever since humans began to live in communities. When someone wanted to exchange a good they had for a good that belonged to a neighbour, they engaged in bartering, offering one valuable good for another of approximately equivalent value. As transactions became more frequent and involved an ever-increasing variety of goods, an alternative to bartering needed to be found to remove the requirement for a coincidence of wants. People turned to a medium of exchange, which was currency. In the third millennium BC, metals began to be used as currency in place of bulkier goods. They had the advantage of being perfectly fungible, and, since of great value, even a small quantity of metal could be used to settle large transactions. A profession was born, which involved keeping, transferring, lending and sometimes producing metal currency.

The bank, a term handed down from the great Italian bankers of the 16th century, initially referred to a money dealer's counter or shop where money was exchanged between the different economic agents, namely, the banker, the depositor and the borrower. As with the tradesman, supplier and customer triptych, the banker initially carried on a business as did any other tradesman. Dealing in money was not fundamentally any different from the trade of other goods, providing gainful employment and serving a social utility.

Over the centuries, as a result of technological progress, the evolution of society and the increasing globalisation of trade, this profession burgeoned into an industry. Bankers, who had simply accepted money in the form of a deposit, held it as they would other wares, and invested it until withdrawn by its original owner, began transforming it.

Transformation by a bank is different from the transformation performed in other industries. In the food or manufacturing industry, processing involves taking a raw material and physically transforming it (such as wheat, turning it into flour) or taking a semi-finished product and transforming it into an object that will be sold at a higher price (such as steel, turning it into a knife). The value added by the industrialist comes from having modified the physical characteristics of the input (raw material). Transformation is a radically different process in the banking industry. The raw material is money, which very early on became metallic so that it could be melted down and was therefore fungible. But, this money — which for about a century has ceased to be either directly or indirectly a physical object, namely a metal — is not physically transformed by the banker. Banking transformation involves taking receipt of an input (money from depositors, invested overnight or for a fixed term) and reusing the same input (money lent to borrowers, generally for a longer term). No physical transformation is involved, money being perfectly fungible at the point of entry and at the point of exit, which is what you might call a transformation over time. The banker's expertise lies not in the tangible but in the temporal.

This essential difference compared with other businesses explains many bank failures. A liquidity risk arises when depositors ask for their money to be returned before borrowers have repaid their loans and there is no other banker, depositor or creditor willing to extend credit. Liquidity management is one of the basics of banking. Through the ages, this has been flouted many a time by bankers, or those professing to be bankers. States, and later central banks, then had to assume the role of lender of last resort to limit the harmful consequences of these bank failures.

The second major risk in banking is credit risk. It arises when the borrower is unable to repay a loan on the due date, notwithstanding the liquidity risk having been ably managed. One of the most subtle aspects of the art of being a banker is knowing how to distinguish between good and bad credit and how to estimate the probability of default by borrowers, in order to compensate statistically for the consequences by applying a margin known as the "credit margin" or "risk premium".

So, by its very nature, banking is a risky business. Liquidity and credit risks reflect the imbalance that exists, in any society, between savers who wish to retain rapid, risk-free access to their deposits and borrowers wanting to finance projects, generally over a longer time horizon, that sometimes fail. Therein lays the usefulness of bankers, the justification for their remuneration and the explanation for the boom in banking during all periods of strong growth when projects are nineteen to the dozen.

For several thousand years, no civilisation has developed without being able to rely on a powerful banking system.

While transformation and providing credit are the essential functions of banking, a plethora of ancillary services have been added over time, stimulated by technological progress and changes in society: advisory, asset and wealth management, foreign exchange, payment solutions (physical, cashless, digital), safe deposit box rental, insurance, etc. These are ancillary services, which may address particular financial concerns and can be extremely lucrative, but are not at the core of banking. Indeed, these services may be provided by entities that are not credit institutions. At a time when the increasing digitalisation of society and changing consumer habits are leading to a very strong acceleration in the digital rollout of these services, to believe that one could, by relying on expertise developed as a service provider, create a bank without mastering liquidity and credit risks is a basic, yet frequent, error. There are already many examples of business failures attributable to this fundamental error, and many more are likely as economic circumstances deteriorate further.

Since the dawn of time, sat behind his counter, the banker has learned to be attentive to the depositor's expectations and to the borrower's projects. To provide the best service while controlling risk exposures, there must be close intimacy between the banker and his customers. The old wooden counter is transformed into a confessional, the banker from a simple tradesman to an adviser. It is easy to see how the very specific role of the banker, which he shares with a few other professions, such as the doctor, adds a new dimension. Customers place their trust in their banker, who assumes the role of trusted third party in today's jargon.

Being called upon to finance major industrial projects as well as the construction of the family home, bankers play a crucial role, like no other, in driving economic growth. They have more information than anyone else about what is going to happen next and more resources than anyone else to decide whether or not to finance a particular project. More often than not, it is they who make it possible for such and such ambition to come to fruition. The banker's role as the lungs of the economy, transforming otherwise idle savings into financing that enables the economy to grow, makes him a player who is often feared but also much in demand in times of crisis. As his very survival depends on his ability to anticipate the future, by drawing on his experience, the banker alone can go out on a limb and take risks that are worth the trouble.

From being the master of liquidity and credit, the banker has become a trusted adviser and, out of necessity, a diviner. That is the evolution of the banking profession since the earliest civilisations.

Banking: New lease of life in the past decade

Comparable in many respects to previous crises, the 2008 crisis was marked in its violence by the accelerating effect of certain of the excesses having derailed the smooth operation of the financial system. Correcting these excesses was one of the main thrusts of the reforms undertaken at international level and in most countries. In addition to the forced departure of the most emblematic figures associated with these malfunctions, the banking profession underwent profound changes.

The first quite striking aspect of this crisis is that responsibilities and risks were spread very widely around the world. This explains why bad credit decisions relating to residential mortgages loans in the far-flung corners of the United States were able to trigger a financial crisis that reverberated around the world. This crisis has often been blamed on securitisation. Loan securitisation did play a role in the transmission, and it was used in connection with the commission of the crime, but it was not the crime itself.

You always have to start from the real world. The starting point is an average American, of rather modest means, who wants to buy a home somewhere in the United States. Perhaps he is relocating to take up a new job, leaving on retirement or simply wants to fulfil the dream of many of his compatriots: to own his own home. A mortgage broker — a profession that has developed strongly in France in recent years — will look for the biggest loan at the best possible rate, acting as a go-between for the buyer and the lender. Typically, this loan will be arranged by a small financial institution, based on a fairly summary risk analysis, the intention being to keep the loan on its books for just a short time. This financial institution is known as the "originator" because it is the original mortgage lender, the starting point in a long chain of decisions that would ultimately lead to the crisis. The originator's goal is to quickly sell this loan to what is known as an "aggregator", which will bundle together a large number of similar mortgage loans granted to a multitude of borrowers across many states, this process being intended to diversify the loan portfolio's risk exposure. As before, the aggregator's goal is not to hold onto these loans to maturity, but to sell the portfolio to investors. The portfolio can be tailored to provide different risk profiles and varying returns. That is where the investment banker steps in. With the help of credit rating agencies, the investment bankers will slice up the portfolio into tranches, each representing a different level of risk: a 1%–2% tranche for the loans expected to be the first to default, a 5% tranche for the loans next expected to experience payment problems, one or two further tranches for lower-risk loans and finally a sizeable tranche consisting of loans for which repayment is near certain. Investors who are not risk-averse and reaching out for high returns will buy the first tranche, also known as the "first loss". At the other extreme, highly risk-averse investors, reassured by the triple-A rating assigned by credit rating agencies, will buy the least risky tranche. This last group of investors, typically the most prudent, will include pension funds and domestic banks located in the four corners of the world. Brokers, originators, aggregators, investment bankers, rating agencies, everyone earns a commission for their excellent work, so that the interest earned by end investors will be far less than what is paid each month by borrowers. Above all, the risk in this chain of transactions has been spread among a large number of investors, some of whom understand their risk exposure, but not all, particularly those buying mortgage-backed securities on the basis of their triple-A rating. When the US real estate market, which until then had been growing steadily but increasingly speculatively, suddenly turns around and default rates start to far exceed their historical trend, and consequently the credit rating agencies' projections, investors are caught wrong-footed. Hedge funds having acquired the first tranches are the first to be affected, but they grasped the risk, this having been integrated into their strategy, and their money came from well-informed investors who could absorb their losses. The crisis becomes global when it affects pension funds or small local banks in Europe or Asia, which simply did not anticipate such high levels of default in the US market and often did not even know what underlying risks lay behind the triple-A rating that frequently was the one factor that governed their investment decision.

That's why there have been endeavours to modify both international and national regulations to prevent repeating this chain of harmful events.

Bankers holding and then securitising loans were directed to retain part of the risk over the term of the transactions. Retaining a vested interest, having skin in the game in the jargon of the trade, avoids a situation where what, from the onset, are bad risks are just passed on to less-well-informed investors. As a result, bankers reverted to exercising the caution from which they should never have departed.

Investors (bankers or insurers) purchasing rated financial securities were directed to apply far more substantial capital charges than before. As a result, buyers will not be found for the most highly rated tranches unless they offer a significant return. Transferring an elevated risk for a microscopic return to an ill-informed financial investor became nearly impossible.

Too many bankers were lured by the hope of easy money and risk-free gains, with often uncritical boards going along "blinded by the science". Regulators have stepped in and imposed requirements for a fit and proper assessment of members of the management body, both in their management function (executive directors) and supervisory function (non-executive directors). In the Old World, company boards were filled by friends who saw it as a social activity or even an opportunity for quid pro quos between people of good company rather than a professional responsibility. These have gradually given way to boards that are more demanding and more aware of the role they have to play in supervising the financiers to whom they entrust the reins of the institution.

Investment bankers have played a central role, snapping up assets, repackaging them and selling them under another name to investors, unconcerned about the ultimate fate of these assets, what mattered being that they be turned over fast enough to unwind positions before problems arose. This has led to very stringent regulations of the remuneration to which these more brilliant than scrupulous intermediaries are entitled. Almost everywhere in the world, the amount of annual bonuses has been capped, typically at around twice the fixed salary. Above all, the requirement has been introduced to spread this variable remuneration over several years. As a result, in the event of a subsequent loss, this remuneration is not paid and, if a banker is found to be at fault, past remuneration can be clawed back.

It is clear that many intermediaries played a role in creating and then transmitting the 2008 crisis. While regulated for a long time on account of their systemic importance, banks failed to exercise self-discipline, prompting supervisory authorities to step in and tighten regulations. These regulations now effectively steer the conduct of business at several levels. In terms of capital, the amount of own funds required in respect of risk exposures has been precisely defined, at levels much higher than under previous regulations, thereby ensuring banks have solid balance sheets. In terms of liquidity risk, the banks' ability to make long-term loans out of funds collected from customers has been severely restricted. As regards customer protection, banks were reminded that they have a duty of care, exercised by providing advice to customers, failing which they expose themselves to sanctions. Finally, financial institutions are now required to effectively prepare for worst-case scenarios leading to failing or likely to fail situations, specifying in these resolution plans (or living wills) whether implementation will be immediate or gradual, temporary or permanent.

More cautious, more resilient, more attentive to their customers, required to draw up living wills, banks have been forced to adopt a different posture since 2008. With bankers having more skin in the game, holding on their books longer risk exposures that are less generously rewarded, forced to wait years to be paid their bonuses and overseen by increasingly demanding boards, the banking profession is now much more closely supervised than it was — to the point that some activities have disappeared altogether.

Chapter 10

Cooperative Banking: A Profession Reinvented by and for Its Customers

An ancient profession, at times feared, at other times envied, shrouded in some mystery on account of the famous banking secrecy, banking was for a long time not accessible to large swathes of the population on account of a potentially bad credit history (small entrepreneurs) or no credit history at all (poorest households). The Age of Enlightenment celebrated reason, which it saw as the power by which humans would improve their condition, and it could not therefore ignore these inequalities, hence the role of the banking profession. For the free spirits who challenged received authority, everyone was master of their destiny, and in finance this meant replacing divine providence by individual providence. This was behind the creation of the first savings and provident institution (*Caisse d'Epargne et de Prévoyance*) in 1818 in Paris. The first institutions of this type were not yet full-fledged banks.

Ultimately, it was the mutualist or cooperative movement — itself a product of humanist ideals of universalism and inclusion that burgeoned in the 18th century — that would inspire the creation of a bank that would be cooperative and accessible to all — a double oxymoron at the time. The creation of a bank that would serve the population at large and not the specific interests of shareholders would draw on the efforts of free spirits from diverse origins, but all driven by the same desire to facilitate the projects of all and sundry, whatever their rung on the social ladder. Coming from very different backgrounds, ardent Catholics with a social fibre, pragmatic Protestants promoting the value of work and its just reward, liberals, sometimes borderline revolutionaries, wishing to open up greater areas of freedom to all and philanthropists convinced that emancipation was within everyone's grasp if empowered would all pursue the same goal.

Two broad approaches, or rather two great human adventures, shaped this veritable reinvention of the centuries-old banking profession.

Observing the plight of farmers in the wake of the 1846 famine, Friedrich-Wilhelm Raiffeisen, the young mayor of Flammersfeld in Prussia, started the Association for Self-procurement of Bread and Fruits (*Verein für Selbstbeschaffung von Brod und Früchten*) that operated a community-built bakery and, a decade later, a rural loan association (*Darlehenskassenverein*) accessible to all. It was administered according to the principles that many financial cooperatives would later adopt: no capital, but in return unlimited liability for its members, unremunerated directors and the allocation of surpluses to an indivisible reserve. Credit societies based on this model flourished and were gradually federated in each of the German states and then at the level of the German Empire when it was established in 1871. There was an evolution in their legal structure, most credit societies progressively going on to have capital contributed by their members and switching to a limited-liability form, the German law enabling in 1889 the liability of cooperative members to be limited to their contribution. Inspired by the Raiffeisen model, Wilhelm Haas started an agricultural purchasers' association (*Verband der hessischen landwirtschaftlichen Konsumvereine*) in Friedberg in 1872 that was joined by other purchasing cooperatives a few months later and went on to start a cooperative bank in 1833 (*Landwirtschaftliche Genossenschaftsbank AG*); while this branch of the cooperative movement enjoyed much success, setbacks ensued and some cooperatives were liquidated, with others integrated into the Raiffeisen banks in 1929. It is the Raiffeisen model that gave birth to the cooperative banks in Germany, the Netherlands and Austria, some of which still carry on business under the Raiffeisen name to this day, but also to the Crédit Agricole in France, whose first local bank was opened in 1885, and the Mouvement Desjardins in Canada, established in 1900. This model was also at the origin of the Crédit Mutuel, whose first local bank was opened in 1882 in Alsace, then part of the German Empire.

Still in Germany, Hermann Schulze-Delitzsch, a lawyer from Saxony, set up a disbursement society (*Vorschussverein*), the precursor of the people's bank (*Volksbank*), in his birthplace in 1850, which advanced money to low-income households and small tradesmen. In keeping with the liberal ideas of its founder, the capital was remunerated according to the risks taken, and directors were also remunerated, but, given the social dimension, the solidarity of the shareholders was unlimited. This model quickly spread in Germany and abroad, inspiring the creation of Banca Popolare di Lodi and Banca Popolare di Milano in Italy, for which the liability of the customer-members was, however, limited to their contributions. This model was embraced by liberal and social Catholics in France. Early success in France was short-lived, however, and there were many failures until the enactment in 1917 of the Clémentel law (*Loi du 13 mars 1917 ayant pour objet l'organisation du crédit au petit et au moyen commerce, à la petite et à la moyenne industrie*), which established a framework for people's banks and allowed these to grant short-term loans and remunerate their directors. Enthusiastic comments at the time show what may have been the first manifestation of a concern for compliance and not just risk management, as promoters of the law stated that credit should not only be granted to those "capable of credit" but above all also to those "worthy of credit".

Cooperative banking was thus born of a general movement that also led to the creation of manufacturing and consumer cooperatives in several European countries and the United States during the 19th century. In each instance, the aim was to combat a form of exclusion by bringing together people to fulfil a want under the best possible conditions, procuring a good or service to which they had no or restricted access. Today, the cooperative banking sector accounts for 20% of bank deposits and loans in Europe. With 700,000 employees, it is one of Europe's biggest employers and taxpayers. In France, two-thirds of bank deposits and loans are managed by mutual banking groups.

It is interesting to understand the main characteristics of this banking model, as opposed to capitalist banking, and how they explain the success of the cooperative model.

First main characteristic: proximity. While all businesses, and all banks, begin on a small scale, usually within a restricted territory, cooperative banks alone have managed to retain this local character, even when they have become large groups on the scale of a country or even the planet. Of the thirty banks on the list of globally systemic banks (G-SIBs), two are French cooperative banking groups (Crédit Agricole and BPCE). These two groups have been able to maintain a highly decentralised organisation, where banks operate within a restricted local perimeter — no larger than a département or region — but with a high degree of autonomy, abiding by a regulatory and supervisory framework decided in common and applied uniformly. This has resulted in a much more granular branch network, which is a major commercial advantage, appealing to a large number of customers, particularly in rural areas. Given the naturally local destination of their investments and the local sourcing of purchases, not to mention locally recruited teams, cooperative banks have become major economic players in their territory.

Second main characteristic: customer focus. Because they were created to address a want felt by certain categories of the population and business community, cooperative banks focused from the onset on these categories. These have included not only economically or socially disadvantaged customers, who are undoubtedly the ones who feel the greatest need for inclusion, but also farmers, shopkeepers or craftsmen. Banks started by groups of individuals to address the needs of specific communities will be considered by all as "their bank" and enjoy an unrivalled love affinity, so that the commonly held perception of cooperative banks is like no other. By their very construct, cooperative banks are able to develop a more tailored range of services for their specific clientele than a bank indiscriminately serving all and sundry.

Third main characteristic: customer–shareholder alignment. As only customers can become shareholders or members of a cooperative bank, they exercise de jure control, ensuring that there is a complete alignment in the interests of the bank's customers and owners. The practice of jacking up prices for certain products or services because there is little competition would not be tolerated by what are not-for-profit institutions dedicated to serving customers to the best of their ability. Apart from the remuneration paid to members (generally strictly regulated by law), the profits generated by a cooperative bank must be used solely to finance its development or strengthen own funds. As a result, while cooperative banks will be less profitable, they are stronger than their competitors — and bound to grow stronger year after year as a result of the steady increase in retained earnings — for the greater benefit of their customers and members.

Fourth main characteristic: lesser risk appetite and long-term vision on account of being owned by their customers. Shielded from excessive pressures on earnings performances — because customer-members have no particular expectations, their overriding concern being the smooth running of their cooperative and its financial solidity — cooperative banks are not encouraged to take significant risks, synonymous with potentially substantial profits but also the risk of abyssal losses. Not being subjected to shareholder pressure as are listed companies that report earnings on a quarterly basis, cooperative banks can pursue a medium- to long-term vision. This explains why they have chosen to develop in sectors that are not very profitable but low risk, such as infrastructure financing. It also explains the stability of their customer base, which does not have to undergo regular reengineering and redistribution exercises to meet what, in the eyes of listed entities, are sacrosanct investor expectations. Activist shareholders do not have much of a hold on cooperative banks either, since member voting rights are based on the democratic principle of one member, one vote, regardless of the number of shares held.

These four characteristics — proximity, customer focus, customer–shareholder alignment and lesser risk appetite/longer-term vision — largely explain the success of cooperative banks that have remained true to their founding principles. It is these same essential characteristics that led them to become universal banks: with no other mission than to serve their member-customers well, cooperative banks have developed a full range of products and services to meet member expectations, sometimes going far beyond the simple management of deposits or the granting of credit. By their very construct, cooperative banks have adopted a relational approach, whereas capitalist banks, just as logically, have sought to develop the most profitable activities, and have therefore embraced a transactional approach to business. After more than a century of cooperative banking, it is clear that the viability of this model is assured. The success of cooperative banks in comparison with their capitalist competitors varies from country to country, mainly due to the regulatory and competitive environment in each country. With the 21st century being so profoundly different, what is the state of play?

It is striking to observe the refocusing of society's concerns on environmental and social issues, on the one hand, and the rejection of globalisation, on the other, castigated for its excesses (by the same token forgetting the economic progress it has brought to the poorest countries and social classes), in favour of a return to spatial proximity.

With regard to this last point, it is clear that being very local, cooperative banks enjoy undeniable advantages, as they have their roots in the territories, participate actively in community life and provide microfinance to customers in one town or several communes at most. These distinctive features have once again found grace in the eyes of rural or neo-rural populations, which should support the banks' development going forward. This is reflected by the evolution in their market share, which has increased to the detriment of the more centralised capitalist banks.

As for concerns over sustainable development, often encapsulated by the ESG triptych, the main features of cooperative banks described above do address the three pillars:

- **Environment:** For customers, the local roots established by cooperative banks are a guarantee they will act responsibly, as concerns over climate change are greater when expected to have proximal consequences as opposed to being a distant threat in the Amazon or Mongolia. The ability to take a long-term view is also a prerequisite for a bank's involvement in financing projects linked to environmental and energy transitions, which are costly undertakings that can only be financed over the long term and with modest prospects in terms of financial profitability, far removed from the expectations of shareholders in listed companies.

- **Social:** The focus of cooperative banks on individuals, professionals and small businesses is in keeping with the ambitions of new generations who, unlike their parents, are less enthralled by the charms of big business and aspire instead to finance their projects as self-entrepreneurs, opening a fair trade business or launching a very small enterprise linked to the social economy. Cooperative banks have long been active in financial education and in combating financial exclusion, which is perceived by customers as indicating an awareness of their wider obligations.

- **Governance:** Appointments at the head of cooperative banks (board of directors, supervisory board, and management team) are decided democratically, based on the principle of one member, one vote. This results in a governance model that is transparent and reassuring, at a time when society, especially in France, is increasingly wary of the rules of the capitalist economy. The commonality of interest between the bank's customers and owners means that the interest of customers is what matters, not the interest of physically distant financial investors.

It is therefore reasonable to think that the cooperative banking model — conceived some two centuries ago and now dominant in certain countries such as France, but considered a little conservative when capitalism was triumphant and globalisation was seen as a positive-sum game — is once again living up to the expectations of a growing number of men and women at the start of the 21st century and set to go from strength to strength throughout the world in the coming decades.

Chapter 11

The Illusion of Control

Are banks responsible?

We know full well the extent to which regulatory measures taken after the Great Recession have affected the banking profession. These regulations are still in force today, or at least in part. One of the characteristics of these regulations is that their elaboration is a very protracted process. Because banks are such important economic agents, responsible for the savings of the population as well as the financing of public and private projects, no authority wants to risk handicapping them by casting doubt about their solidity in the eyes of depositors, nor do they want to hinder their ability to support the economic recovery. Each regulatory change is therefore carefully weighed up, discussed at length between the banks and the governments at the country level, and then at the international level in the case of G-SIBs.

This takes time, after which implementation is also very often a long-drawn-out process. Rules imposing an increase in own funds must allow banks time to build these up themselves or to bide their time and issue shares when there is keen investor appetite. Measures designed to modify credit policies must come into force without scuppering operations under discussion. Also, any changes must be coordinated across the branch network. As a result, it is not uncommon for a package of measures to take ten or fifteen years to come into force, long after the crisis that inspired the new regulations.

Several of the measures taken over the last ten years or so have been aimed primarily at making bank managers more accountable. It has to be said that, during the subprime crisis, bank executives did not distinguish themselves, their grasp of risks and sense of responsibility being found wanting when disaster struck. They were quick to go cap in hand to central banks and governments to have them provide liquidity, buy up impaired assets and shore up own funds, in short, asking them to assume responsibilities that were the banks'.

A number of important decisions were taken regarding the accountability of board members, senior executives and line executives.

In the case of banks governed by the Capital Requirements Directive,[1] appointments to management bodies must be approved by the competent central bank or supervisory authority, applying what are now stringent rules limiting the number of directorships and ensuring sufficient time is devoted to the performance of their functions in the bank. These requirements pursue different objectives: limit conflicts of interest in the first case, ensure active involvement in the bank's supervision in the second case. Furthermore, in approving appointments, the central bank or supervisory authority considers whether members of management bodies possess sufficient knowledge, skills and experience to perform their duties, with banks being required to provide adequate training. With these changes, the intention of the authorities is to emphasise the importance given to management functions (executive management committee) and supervisory functions (board of directors, supervisory board). The central bank or supervisory authority may refuse or withdraw approval from any member of a management body if they fail to discharge their responsibilities in a satisfactory manner, though such a sanction is very rare.

Recent regulations have placed bankers squarely before their responsibility, as they have had more concrete implications, affecting in particular their remuneration. As a rule, members of the supervisory function should be compensated only with a fixed remuneration. Note that a fixed amount per working hour or day, even if the time to be reimbursed is not predefined, is considered a fixed remuneration. A high-risk operation generating significant revenues on inception, as is the case with many market operations, such as securitisations, may not lead to the payment of a bonus or additional remuneration in any form to board members. As for executive committee members, line executives and identified staff having a

---

[1] Text largely based on Article 1 of Capital Requirements Directive.

material impact on the institution's risk profile, their variable remuneration must be strictly supervised and vest over a period of years, such that payments can be suspended and even clawed back if there are ex-post risk adjustments before remuneration has vested. Furthermore, to ensure adequate segregation of duties, as a rule, the chairman of the management body in its supervisory function of an institution must not simultaneously exercise the functions of a chief executive officer within the same institution. The days of all powerful bosses and high-flying bankers paid astronomic remunerations are a thing of the past.

These changes certainly ensure greater responsibility on the part of the players involved, and all in all on the part of the banks. However, it has to be said that for the time being this concerns only European banks. There is no certainty that these regulations will be applied in the United States or in Asia. Also, the rules are different for activities bordering on banking but also likely to manage savings and to finance the economy, such as asset management and insurance.

The regulations requiring banks to retain part of the risk, when structuring complex transactions sold on to buy-to-hold investors, have already been mentioned. Aligning the long-term interests of banks and investors has also contributed to a more responsible approach to banking. Alongside regulations having had virtuous effects, the negative impact of numerous other rules restraining banking practices, particularly within the euro area, does need to be highlighted. When Danièle Nouy joined the European Central Bank in 2014 as Chair of the Supervisory Board of the Single Supervisory Mechanism, she announced that "we will be a tough supervisor and will at all times strive to be fair and even-handed in our actions"[2], and she would later add "intrusive". While the need for a fair and even-handed supervisor goes without saying, and being tough can be explained by the excesses observed a few years ago, which played a major role in the Great Recession, it is more surprising to be warning banks to expect intrusive supervision.

What this intrusion actually means is plain to see in the numerous regulations as well as in the very extensive interpretation of the regulations themselves, which have become the hallmarks of banking supervision in the European Union. Over the last 10 years or so, when considered

---

[2]Danièle Nouy (2014) Chair of the Supervisory Board of the Single Supervisory Mechanism, keynote address at the inauguration of the European Central Bank's new supervisory responsibilities.

individually, a series of generally well-intentioned rules have been introduced to regulate borrower profiles, borrowing limits and loan terms, sometimes the level of the bank's remuneration and almost always the provisions recognised in P&L, the names given to products and wording of accompanying disclaimers (which are getting longer and longer and are therefore skipped over), the management of capital resources and their allocation between the different business lines and countries where they operate, etc. These general rules, which are added to month after month, limit the development of banks by defining boundaries more and more precisely, not only creating ex nihilo a systemic risk discussed later on but also lessening the banks' sense of responsibility.

Reduced to the role of mere executors of strategies devised by this or that authority (engaged in *de facto* management, but neither possessing the means nor, above all, having been given this mandate), banks are increasingly infantilised. And, as is taught in law schools, infants cannot be held responsible for their actions.

This has led to a proliferation of regulations, itself the consequence of ever-expanding statute books, written in haste in response to this or that unfortunate event.

The result is a maze of texts likely to confuse and confound, when these should be a pathway to responsible banking practices. This ever-growing corpus is being applied by central bank teams at country and EU levels in a very "intrusive" way, as announced in 2014. What ensues is the micromanagement of banks by supervisors. It matters not the sector of activity, micromanagement is known to be extremely counterproductive.

In particular, in the present case, it stems from a misconception: the function of supervisors is not to micromanage or macromanage banks. If they do, which is all too often the case, it lessens the banks' sense of responsibility. This was certainly not the regulators' objective, but that is the outcome.

Have banks had their wings clipped?

The strategic plans regularly published by major competitors can but pique the curiosity of a banker. Each time, the impression is of rereading more or less the same text. In France, does this come from bank managers being cast in the same mould? Is it because the consulting firms used by the big banks are often the same? It would be an insult to everyone's intelligence to see these as the only explanations. The fact is that, over the years, regulations governing the practice of banking have become so dense and detailed that they leave little room for human intelligence and for managers to show much imagination.

Prudential regulation, at work for several decades now and international in scope, is the most striking example. To ensure that risks taken by banks are covered by a reasonable percentage of their capital, so that an accident does not systematically have a negative impact on depositors or lead to taxpayers eventually being called to the rescue, a capital measurement system for each bank, commonly referred to as the Basel Capital Accord or Basel I, was introduced in 1988 by the Basel Committee. To arrive at increasingly precise capital adequacy requirements for risk exposures, the initial text evolved little by little, with the release of Basel II, then III and finally IV. Over time, the framework has become more prescriptive and has been refined to address different types of activities and borrowers. Facing intense competition, and judged on their ability to generate a satisfactory return on capital employed, banks have naturally adjusted commercial policies, and in particular the interest margins charged to borrowers, to reflect regulatory capital requirements. What has followed is that differences in the positioning of banks relative to each other have gradually faded. There's no need to look any further for the reasons behind the gradual demise of these small and medium-sized banks, which had historically specialised in a particular customer segment, geographical catchment area or economic sector. What emerged were banks that were all rather similar, with no marked differentiation and, above all, no perceived decisive competitive advantage for customers.

Regulations are also sometimes used to impose very stringent restrictions, even to explicitly prohibit certain banking activities. Extensive use of this possibility has been made by states wielding significant financial or legal clout because of their strategic importance for any bank with global ambitions, or because of the long arm of their law. The United States, for example, has sought increasingly to bring within the scope of its own laws international transactions that it wants to ban, arguing that the country's currency was used for these transactions. In particular, transactions with countries placed under embargo by the US administration, those undertaken on behalf of businesses or individuals considered hostile by the US administration, fund transfers susceptible of contributing to the financing of groups identified by the US administration as being involved in terrorism and organised crime are banned, concerning not just US banks but also international banks. Russia and China have done much as the United States, not by weaponising their currency, as they could not, but by conditioning access to their domestic market to international groups toeing the line. Today, a bank with even the smallest of international operations will have a strategy towards Iran, Crimea, Hong Kong or projects in Russia much as those of other banks. It is difficult to find any bank prepared to do things otherwise. Humanitarian aid organisations active in Syria, for example, have complained bitterly about this rigid mindset.

In France, very few of the lowest-income households have access to credit. Debt becomes a reality upon being overdrawn at the bank, often unbeknown to them and almost always unwillingly. At that point, all kinds of charges pile up, sometimes setting off a spiral of overindebtedness. Consumer associations were the first to raise awareness of this toxic phenomenon before politicians took up the fight. This led to a significant reduction in amounts charged by banks for unauthorised overdrafts. Of course, this development is to be welcomed, but it will certainly not make it easier for the most vulnerable in society to obtain banking facilities. This does beg the question of why, more than in other countries, access to credit in France is limited to a certain category of the population. The very unpleasant truth is that, while the usury rate, which is much lower than in most of France's neighbours, has certainly prevented a drift towards subprime lending, it is also preventing banks from striking a balance between margins generated from lending to these vulnerable customers and the inevitably high cost of risk on this type of lending. In France, it is the regulations — highly protective of consumers — that dictate the banks' policy towards the poorest customers.

In terms of business financing, the impact of the measures taken by various authorities to protect the environment is also having a huge impact. Financing extended for coal and even oil extraction is becoming increasingly limited, to the extent that some businesses operating in these sectors, though essential to today's economy, are finding it difficult to obtain the bank financing they are looking for. On the other hand, the financing of renewable energies is being encouraged by subsidies and incentives of all kinds around the world. The result is a proliferation of industrial players and projects that are not always economically or technologically profitable and can only be financed because tax or regulatory advantages give them preferential access to banks. As seen in Spain, it is only a matter of time before this artificial bubble bursts and bankruptcies follow. In the meantime, banks, reluctantly or willingly, are all applying the same commercial policies.

One of the major innovations of recent years has been the ultra-accommodating monetary policies adopted by the central banks of the world's three major financial blocks (United States, European Union and Japan). When central banks set zero interest rates (ZIRP), even negative interest rates (NIRP), this will obviously have a major impact on commercial banks, affecting the cost of the resources they transform. The first effect, which was the goal of central banks, is a much greater propensity on the part of commercial banks to lend, even to businesses with doubtful repayment capacity. Another effect, less well anticipated, is that deposits are not a sought-after resource since they cannot be transformed profitably. Though deposit-taking had been one of the strengths of commercial banks, this activity ended up being fobbed off to new players. Commercial banks are only too happy to refinance themselves at negative interest rates at the central bank, while falling over each other to distribute loans, exposing themselves to a systemic risk further down the road. Be that as it may, commercial banks end up pursuing similar strategies because central bank monetary policy rules are pushing them in the same direction.

Turning to activities in the capital markets, the phenomenon is similar. Long gone are the days of the Glass–Steagall Act, which saw some banks specialise in investment banking activities and others in so-called commercial banking. Since the Great Recession, most US investment banks have been acquired by commercial banks. The remaining stand-alone Wall Street banks took licences from the Federal Reserve to allow them to take deposits from the public, converting into commercial banks. The diversity that used to characterise banking activities carried on by leading American institutions has largely disappeared. Goldman Sachs, the epitome of Wall Street investment banking, is now expanding into retail banking through a dedicated brand, Marcus, and signed a partnership with Apple, ranging from co-branded consumer credit cards to savings accounts. Its strategic ambitions are not far removed from those of JPMorgan, now JP Morgan Chase following the merger of several large US banks, including Chase Manhattan Bank, one of the oldest US commercial banks. This convergence of strategies is the consequence of the unification of regulations to such a high level of granularity that the chief executive of Goldman Sachs has no more room to manoeuvre than his counterpart at JP Morgan.

All these examples drawn from recent experience, and which are still at play, underline the increasing difficulty for a bank to adopt a different policy from that of its competitors. Of course, there are good policies and not-so-good policies, but in this business where time is of the essence, history is the ultimate judge. Is the infantilisation of banks by their supervisory authority a guarantee of success? Does reducing the capacity for initiative to almost nothing bring progress? Clearly, denying all entrepreneurial freedom to institutions such as banks, whose essential social role is to support entrepreneurs, is to the detriment of two objectives: the diversity of the financial system (and therefore its structural soundness) and the healthy competition from which consumers and businesses could otherwise benefit (in turn driving economic growth).

Are banks dangerous?

Banking regulations lacking in proportionality, addressing in great minutia the core business of banking instead of simply setting a framework within which banks can operate, inexorably lead each bank to adopt the same commercial strategy. If this proves harmful, all the banks will be exposed to the same, therefore, systemic, risk. The volume of transactions influenced in this way by the regulator or supervisor is all the greater because it concerns the very core of the business, more specifically lending. This heightens the systemic risk and will amplify the magnitude of any crisis.

Banks may also be more tempted to circumvent regulations restricting their core business. The more specific and prescriptive the regulations become in their minutia, the more ways the banks have of circumventing restrictions. Creative ways of circumventing regulations will fuel systemic risk until the resulting bubble bursts. The subprime crisis is a good example of how regulations were circumvented in the pursuit of short-term profitability through the securitisation of high-risk mortgages.

To avoid global banking crises, it would be desirable for banking regulations to be more like the Highway Code, setting out the rules defining a code of conduct and speed limits without indicating the destination, so that regulations remain relevant over time.

Reaching out for higher returns in the short term came at a steep cost for the banks and all of the world's economies. A wave of populism, surfing on the crisis, swept across the world. Admittedly, this did not lead to a world war like the Great Depression. Nevertheless, the political risk increased after the subprime crisis, as shown by the Yellow Vests movement in France and the rise of extremist parties across Europe and in the United States. For the European Union, the subprime crisis was a watershed moment, just like the Great Depression seventy years earlier.

When the COVID-19 crisis came along, European economies would have been in a far better place had it not been for the subprime crisis. Budget cuts in Italy and France, for example, had led to a drastic reduction in the number of intensive care beds, which led to lockdowns for lack of any other means of managing peaks in the epidemic. In France, the two lockdowns in 2020 came at a huge socio-economic cost. The country's gross domestic product shrank by 8.3% in 2020. Healthcare workers came into the pandemic worn out by months of strikes that disrupted public transport at the end of 2019 and in the first months of 2020. The strikes were over the government's pension reform, made necessary by the subprime crisis. As for shopkeepers, they were already on their knees financially after the Yellow Vests movement, with large-scale weekly protests that lasted for months. This movement was also brought about by the impoverishment of the population in the wake of the 2008 crisis.

Part IV

Seven Proposals for a Healthy Recovery

Crescentia sana in mundo sano[*]

Ancient wisdom has bequeathed us this precept: "A healthy mind in a healthy body". This apparently simple rule of life seems to be poorly applied in today's society.

For individuals, life expectancy in the developed world increased more than ever before in the 20th century, but these years gained in old age are not always enviable in terms of moral or physical health. Even among the younger generations, physical condition in the 2020s is not the same as that of our forebears who lived in the fresh air and engaged in physical activity daily. Our civilisation is also proud of the advances in education. Yet, for all these efforts, the outcome sometimes leaves a bitter taste: incivilities have never been so numerous, and pupils having come out of the public education system, steeped in republican and secular values, have committed morally reprehensible acts. The ancient ideal, which

---

[*]Healthy growth in a healthy world, inspired by the Latin phrase *Mens sana in corpore sano*, meaning a healthy mind in a healthy body, which comes from Satire X of the Roman poet Juvenal.

inspired the Enlightenment and the French Revolution, and should have brought us closer, seems ever more difficult to achieve.

At the collective level, of particular interest since we are talking about the economy and a global crisis, the case can be made that this ideal should be transposed, adapted to read "healthy growth in a healthy world". By applying this simple precept to society as a whole in an increasingly globalised world, the message is that today's disruptions — affecting the climate, social order, financial stability, and migration flows — are of our making. If the world is slightly out of kilter, it is up to us to fix the problems, to change the world before it spins off its axis.

For a healthy world, read a sustainable world as defined decades ago. Healthy growth is sustainable, responsible and thoughtful growth. It is not anarchic growth, nor the lethargic growth advocated by some. Growth being what it is, it needs financing and therefore the banks. How can banks play their role, which since the dawn of time has been to accompany the world's evolution, here and now and in so doing make tomorrow's world a healthier place?

Healthy, therefore sustainable, that "meets the needs of the present without compromising the ability of future generations to meet their own needs".[1]

---

[1] United Nations Brundtland Commission (1987) *Report of the World Commission on Environment and Development: Our Common Future*. http://www.un-documents.net/our-common-future.pdf.

Chapter 12

Rethinking Public Health Policy

Laden with debt as a result first of the 2008 crisis and then of the pandemic, European states will have to draw all the lessons from the inquiries into COVID-19, its effects on the economy and its implication for the public health system, and come up with lasting solutions for the 21st century. Of course, the emergency measures come at a high financial cost, to which governments are resigned in the short term. Over the medium term, however, the financial resources to provide curative treatments addressing the deterioration in the health of the general population, on the one hand, and quick fix solutions for the planet's problems, on the other hand, will simply be prohibitive. The economic cycle initiated by the Industrial Revolution in Great Britain in the 18th century needs to give way to a new economic cycle. Most of the economic progress, such as one understands this term, over the last three centuries has come from that revolution. However, the Industrial Revolution does seem to have reached its limits and the next chapter in human progress needs to be written. Even though there is now a better understanding of our planet, the challenge is enormous.

And the same is true, surprisingly, of our bodies. The COVID-19 crisis, when hospitals were overwhelmed, has highlighted the need for immediate action to improve the health of the general population, which has been undermined by contemporary lifestyles, and reduce air pollution, whose effects on health are well documented.

The environment and human health will demand changes on the same scale as those brought about by the Internet revolution. After the digital transition, structural, radical changes will be needed to the way in which we think about the environment and our health.

Will there even be one EU member state with the means to fund an overextended healthcare system treating Europeans suffering from malnutrition, ingesting products containing glyphosate,[2] for example, when they think they follow a healthy diet, and breathing highly polluted air when they are told Europe is the best place on earth?

According to the French National Cancer Institute, there were 382,000 new cases of cancer in Metropolitan France in 2018. That's several times the number of COVID-19 cases in 2020 and 2021! Since 2004, cancer has been the leading cause of premature death in France. It is estimated that there are currently 3.8 million people in France who have been diagnosed with cancer.[3] Faced with this explosion in the number of cases, often linked to lifestyles, the economic and social paradigm needs to change.

For several decades, we have imported many of the goods we consume from China, but ignored traditional Chinese medicine, though it is a complete medical system used for more two thousand years, which could be an alternative or a complement to our more recent Western medicine. Of course, many Europeans already have recourse to pharmacopoeia, based on mixtures composed essentially of plants, or acupuncture sessions. However, the French health system does not recognise or reimburse these treatments, which have been tried and tested for many centuries, are almost all derived from nature and therefore inexpensive. The intention is not to pit the Western medical system against China's, but for traditional medicine to complement mainstream healthcare. No question of pitting natural science against chemistry or physics. Speaking at a conference in Singapore, World Health Organization Director-General Margaret Chan said the sustainability of health services is a concern around the world, and one way to reduce the burden on health services is traditional Chinese medicine, making the point that, "I am Chinese, and I have used traditional Chinese medicine throughout my lifetime. I have no doubt that these preparations soothe, treat many common ailments, and relieve pain. But if

---

[2]Glyphosate is a broad-spectrum herbicide, currently with the highest production volume of all herbicides. It is used in more than 750 different products for agriculture, forestry, urban and home applications. It has been classified as "probably carcinogenic to humans" (Group 2A). www.thelancet.com/oncology, Vol. 16, May 2015.

[3]www.fondation-arc.org/le-cancer-en-chiffres.

I have a bad toothache, I go to the dentist."[4] A sign of the priorities, China joined the World Trade Organization in 2001; traditional Chinese medicine was recognised by the World Health Organization in 2019.[5] Recognition and supervision of traditional Chinese medicine would improve health-care, as well as control the quality of the products consumed and the hygiene of the interventions, notably acupuncture, whose therapeutic virtues are unquestionable.

The number of overweight people could be reduced by an effective public policy providing nutritional and sports support for the people concerned. More targeted redistribution of wealth would enable families on very low incomes to feed their children more healthily. As we saw earlier, obesity often begins in childhood. More body-awareness education, or more restrictive regulations dealing with the systematic addition of sugar to food, could reduce the number of diabetes sufferers. Sugar is one of the worst enemies of the 21st-century man.

Being healthy leads to subjective well-being, which can be expected to boost confidence and, in turn, economic activity. The OECD has developed the Better Life Index,[6] which is all about life satisfaction. Surveys were conducted in 38 countries and measured subjective well-being across eleven dimensions: housing, income and wealth, work and job quality, health, knowledge and skills, environmental quality, subjective well-being, safety, work-life balance, social connections, civil engagement.

As Leonardo da Vinci repeatedly explained to Francis I, the education of the population is essential to a country's social and economic well-being. To seek employment and keep abreast in the global economic race, studying and constant up-skilling are the answer. On average, the French can expect to spend 16.6 years in formal education from the ages of 5–39, one year less than the OECD average. The reason for this is simple, if surprising, for while

---

[4] Chan, M. (2016) *The contribution of traditional Chinese medicine to sustainable development*, keynote address at the International Conference on the Modernization of Traditional Chinese Medicine.

[5] World Health Organization (WHO) member states adopted the eleventh revision of the International Statistical Classification of Diseases and Related Health Problems (ICD-11) on 25 May 2019. Historically, traditional Chinese medicine (TCM) was excluded from the ICD system. Including TCM in the ICD-11 is not only a landmark for the ICD but also a milestone for TCM; source: https://pubmed.ncbi.nlm.nih.gov/31933225/.

[6] https://www.oecd.org/social/the-path-to-happiness-lies-in-good-health-and-a-good-job-the-better-life-index-shows.htm.

more years are spent in primary to tertiary education, the French receive less training over their working life. By comparison, on average, Italians and Americans spend 17 years in education, Germans and Norwegians 18 years, and the Dutch, Swedes and Belgians 19 years.[7]

Education and environmental quality are both priorities. Logically enough, France ranks below the average of the 38 OECD countries when it comes to the environmental quality. On average, 84% of people in OECD countries said they were satisfied with water quality. On the other hand, air pollution in urban areas is at levels that, in time, will lead to excess mortality. PM2.5 refers to tiny particulate matter small enough to be inhaled into the deepest part of the lungs, reducing life expectancy. In France, average PM2.5 concentration in the air reaches 11.4 micrograms per cubic metre. According to the WHO guidelines, the annual average concentration of PM2.5 should not exceed 10 micrograms per cubic metre.

This is a topical issue. According to Swiss researcher Mario Rohrer, his studies suggest that SARS-CoV-2 was already present in Europe at the end of 2019, "While the sharp increase in morbidity and mortality was only recorded in spring 2020 in Paris and London. [...] these increases in cases followed phases where the levels of fine particles in the air were higher." The research shows that "Acute concentrations of fine particles, especially those smaller than 2.5 μm, cause inflammation of the respiratory, pulmonary and cardiovascular tracts and thicken the blood. In combination with a viral infection, these inflammatory factors can lead to a serious progression of the disease. Inflammation also promotes the attachment of the virus to cells."[8]

Public hospitals are suffering from a lack of resources as much as from their internal organisation. In France, and particularly in Paris, overcrowded emergency departments expose patients with serious conditions to a life-threatening risk. Many observers think it would be judicious to set up a rapid and efficient patient triage system so that urgent cases can be dealt with expeditiously.

It has been established that when there is an emergency, the distance to hospital is associated with an increase in the risk of patient mortality. In the case of Paris, closing the Hôtel-Dieu or other hospitals will not improve healthcare for the population.

---

[7] https://www.oecd-ilibrary.org/education/education-at-a-glance_19991487.
[8] Rohrer, M. B. and Flahaul, A. (2020) *COVID-19: Air Quality Influences the Pandemic*. University of Geneva, Communication Department.

Let's not give in to sometimes misleading comparisons. Public hospitals are not businesses. Patients cannot become customers, because they do not pay for the services they come for, and competition does not come into play. Hospitals cannot therefore be run like businesses, or else they will become a factory, with performances measured and paid by the task. Healthcare staff would become assembly line workers. It would be insulting to their expertise, dehumanising for them and the patients, and ineffective in terms of patient outcome.

Providing healthcare is much more complex than selling your run-of-the-mill product or service: dispensing health advice, listening to patients and providing psychological support are just as necessary as medical examinations. An illness must be tackled on all fronts, especially in a society where psychosomatic illnesses such as autoimmune diseases are on the increase. Taking the time to examine all the medical tests, getting to know the patient's health history, medical antecedents and risk factors, listening to the patient, explaining the ins and outs of their illness, giving the patient the hope and strength to overcome the illness, and advising them on the basis of who they are as human beings are crucial to their recovery. With a little more communication and slightly fewer technical examinations or drug prescriptions, the pharmaceutical industry would probably make less money, but the likelihood of patients being cured would increase thanks to truly tailor-made treatments. You cannot put a price per word on what the doctor has to say, for it is priceless. More's the pity, as a favourable patient outcome depends on those few words.

By the same logic, more beds are needed for follow-up care and rehabilitation (for example, after surgery or curative/acute care). Most of these beds were eliminated after the 2008 financial crisis. How many Parisians have a lift in their building and the space they need to return home in a wheelchair after a major operation? What about single people on low incomes? How can they organise themselves when they are sent home immediately after an operation? How do patients feel when brutally discharged from the hospital because of a lack of resources, despite their medical and psychological condition justifying they stay an extra night? Have they not paid hefty social security contributions deducted at source in the hope of getting quality care when the time came? And imagine how healthcare workers feel when they are forced to do this because of a lack of resources in a country as rich and civilised as France. It is this kind of frustration that you hear when doctors and staff down their stethoscopes for placards brandished noisily in street protests. The frustrated patients, on the other hand, suffer in silence.

Even if, on paper, there is a possibility for GPs to see seriously ill patients in their own homes, given the shortage of private practitioners, it is very difficult for them to organise visits to these seriously ill patients, moreover for totally inadequate fees. If no new beds are opened quickly, one solution could be to offer young doctors who are going into hospital medicine the possibility of providing medical home visits under training programmes for a few years, as part of their hospital induction.

Successive cost-cutting plans, based on the misguided assumption that a public hospital is to be run like a business, have only made the situation worse. Hospitals in Paris are often in a state of disrepair: doctors are forced to work in temperatures of over 40°C during the increasingly frequent heat waves, as wards are not fitted with air conditioning. No matter the position, decent pay and working conditions are essential to recruit and then retain staff. Health workers are in constant contact with people in distress: if they themselves are worn out physically by their working conditions and psychologically for no longer being able to treat patients as they see fit, or because profitability is the be-all and end-all, they will not be able to provide proper care. It is striking that the life expectancy of doctors is lower than that of the population entrusted to their care. The only logic of a public hospital should be to cater effectively to patient needs. There can be no purely accounting logic in an activity where the aim is to understand, to treat ill health and its recurrence. Providing care is enough of a challenge without adding even more red tape and/or having to make do with an underperforming IT system, the complexity of which simply reflects the inadequacy of the accounting principles imposed from above.

Businesses can also play a role in curbing the pressure on the healthcare system, which is then better able to focus on serious and unavoidable cases. By getting more involved, employers can ensure that their employees enjoy a healthier, more pleasant life, and therefore are more productive. If the roles of occupational health doctors and social workers at companies were strengthened, this would make it possible to intervene quickly, for example, in cases of moral harassment, before it triggers chronic pathologies that are rarely reversible. The pressure on the healthcare system would be reduced, as would the human and financial costs. Personalised support for an employee in recovery, for example, providing therapeutic part-time work, would help him avoid feeling redundant, isolated or rejected by society, helping him get back on his feet more quickly. The psychological factor is crucial in any illness, and the way in which each company treats any member of staff in ill health plays a central role in the recovery process. Hence the vital role of occupational health doctors, who can explain to an employer how best to integrate a fragile employee and help him overcome or live with his illness.

Chapter 13

Repositioning Europe Centre Stage in the World

The COVID-19 pandemic has intensified the economic war between the United States and China. It was waged with great fanfare by Donald Trump, and is likely to be pursued with less fanfare but just as much determination by Joe Biden. The urgency is there: the United States wants to take advantage of its status as the world's leading power, while it still is, to open new rounds of negotiations with China, Russia and their allies. The goal is to curb Chinese expansion. Given the acceleration of China's powering up post-COVID, time is of the essence. For the first time since 1945, the United States may no longer be the world leader. It is not just an economic war: what is at stake is global influence, pitting a Chinese-style totalitarian hegemony against an American-style democratic hegemony. The competition is not just economic and military, it is diplomatic and ideological.

At the onset, the United States was isolationist through and through, determined that it should have with foreign nations "as little connection as possible,"[1] focused instead on the westward expansion and exploitation of its territory, much as China until Deng Xiaoping. It was the two world wars (into which the Americans were dragged by Europe) that led the United States to evolve towards a hegemonic position. We can speak of a cold war between the United States and China because the two powers are not in a win-win situation: any ground lost by one is gained by the other. Russian GDP was just 40% of US GDP at the height of their Cold War.

---

[1] George Washington's 1796 dictum.

Chinese GDP has expanded to 70% of US GDP, but when China joined the World Trade Organization (WTO), it was just 10% of US GDP. Comparing the three countries from a different angle, demographics, Russia was ranked tenth in the world with 144.5 million inhabitants in 2018, China first with 1.393 billion inhabitants and the United States was fourth with 328.21 million, some way behind the European Union's 27 countries with 448 million and far ahead of Russia.

China's economic, military and ideological aggression is not just rhetoric, but a reality and almost a necessity given its size. The fact that the United States perceives China as a threat is not absurd, and does not stem solely from the need to have a designated rival, a foreign enemy responsible for all the country's internal woes, but for whom they would not be. China constitutes an economic, technological, diplomatic and military challenge. The BATX are taking on the GAFAM. The United States is at war, on the defensive against China in absolutely all fields of human endeavour.

With China a step ahead of the game with its vaccine diplomacy, the riposte of the United States came on 12 March 2021, at the first meeting of the Quadrilateral Security Dialogue (Quad), the informal strategic forum bringing together the United States, India, Japan and Australia, when it was announced these countries would finance, manufacture and distribute at least 1 billion "safe and effective" doses of coronavirus vaccine to much of Asia by the end of 2022.[2] The reference to "safe and effective" vaccine doses is a barely veiled allusion to the Chinese vaccine, which had not been authorised for marketing by the European Medicines Agency (EMA), among others, for lack of published trial data. What was striking at the time was that China had vaccinated fewer people inside China than outside. Genuine vaccine diplomacy or clinical trials: it is anyone's guess.

For the time being, the European Union remains a mere observer of the cold war between the United States and China, even though President Joe Biden has been trying to enlist its support. Obviously, Chinese values correspond much less to European values than American values. Euro-Americans have been the largest pan-ethnic group in the United States for centuries, establishing what some have called a plutocratic circle.

---

[2] "The Quad committed to delivering up to one billion doses to ASEAN (Association of Southeast Asian Nations), the Indo-Pacific and beyond by the end of 2022," US National Security Advisor Jake Sullivan said shortly after the virtual summit.

Nevertheless, the American principle of extraterritoriality is highly coercive, even punitive, for European countries. The fines imposed under this questionable principle, which is by definition hegemonic, have cost European businesses tens of billions of euros. This has led to a loss of competitiveness compared with their American counterparts. This is clearly a source of friction. One can argue that the apparently neutral attitude of the European Union makes sense right now, for while Joe Biden's America has more values in common with Europe than Donald Trump's America, there is no guarantee it will share the spoils if the United States does eventually prevail against China. If the European Union steps into the ring, it will take all the hits without necessarily having much to show for the pain. Also, Europe is not necessarily well disposed towards the supremacist attitude of the United States and its readiness to take on all countries threatening its economic success.

Can the Americans win the economic and ideological war against China and preserve their world leadership? A large part of the world considers China's future domination to be inevitable. Americans, on the other hand, are firm believers in the principle that "where there's a will, there's a way".

The Chinese, quite simply, believe that they are reclaiming what is rightfully theirs, the central place that history and demography have given them for centuries. At different times, China has been called the Middle or Central Kingdom, implying its superior role as the centre of civilisation or even the world. For China, the 19th and 20th centuries were just unfortunate, temporary mishaps. China claims that it is not being attacked for what it does, but simply for what it is, a country in the process of becoming the world's leading power once again. In reality, what they do and what they are now constitute a threat to the United States.

As in any cold war, the populations of the warring countries are encouraged to embrace a very negative perception of the enemy. Since Donald Trump's presidency, China has been seen as a hostile power by most Americans. In general, particularly since the pandemic, China's image has become more negative throughout the Western world.

Donald Trump was relentless in his attacks on China. He referred to COVID-19 as the "Chinese virus", which was politically astute, and not without some justification. It is not the first time a country has been stigmatised: the Great Influenza went by the common misnomer of the Spanish flu, for it did not originate in Spain. However, apart from Donald Trump, no one has dared to call this the Chinese virus or the

Chinese flu, even though it originated in Wuhan. Fear of upsetting the future masters of the world? The European Union has shown an abundance of caution in all matters: had the roles been reversed, would China have shown the slightest hesitation? In his inaugural speech, President Biden took up the torch of the ideological and trade war against China, talking of America's role in the world, and promising to be more effective than his predecessor.

Outside the United States, the Trump presidency badly tarnished the image of American democracy. The final weeks of the Trump presidency were marred by the assault on the Capitol, the previously unassailable symbol of American democracy. That the Capitol should be invaded in the 21st century, after having been impregnable for two centuries, says a lot about the Trump presidency and the state of the country. It is hard to go on giving lessons in democracy after this. The ideological decline of the United States and the collapse of its previously flourishing economy as a result of COVID-19 explain the rising tensions between the United States and China.

In China, the two-term limit for the presidency was abolished when the constitution was reformed in 2018, aligning the presidency with the position of Chinese Communist Party General Secretary, which does not have term limits. Xi Jinping, who holds both positions as well as being the Chairman of the Central Military Commission, was 70 when he was re-elected President in 2023. Having set himself up for life, he has strengthened his grip over a one-party state that seems to have turned the page on the pandemic. Following this constitutional change, China has become much tougher, more authoritarian and totalitarian. Yet, Deng Xiaoping, who was behind the economic reforms after the Maoist era, warned that "First of all, it is not good to have an over-concentration of power. It hinders the practice of socialist democracy and of the Party's democratic centralism, impedes the progress of socialist construction and prevents us from taking full advantage of collective wisdom."[3] The era of the "Little Helmsman", as Deng Xiaoping was known, seems a long way away. Nowadays, it is the life of the "Great Helmsman" — the name given to Chairman Mao Zedong during the Great Leap Forward — that tends to be celebrated. For China, the American economic and political model is in decline. The Chinese authorities have used American criticism very

---

[3] Xiaoping, D. (1980) *On the Reform of the System of Party and State Leadership*. https://www.marxists.org/reference/archive/deng-xiaoping/1980/220.htm.

skilfully to revive Chinese nationalism. Since the start of the pandemic in Wuhan, the rhetoric against the United States has become even more virulent. The best defence for the Chinese has been attack. A mea culpa would indeed have been very surprising. It follows that the Chinese have an increasingly negative view of the Western world in general.

This hardening can also be explained by the fact that while China is grappling with food and energy security, it is also being criticised by a large proportion of young people in Asia. The Milk Tea Alliance, or how a hashtag turned into a global democracy movement, was launched on social networks by netizens. It has nothing to do with the Tea Party in the United States. Chinese traditionally drink green tea without milk, a symbol of their austerity, whereas in Tibet, Taiwan, Hong Kong, Myanmar and Thailand, milk or condensed milk is added to the tea. Many assume that adding milk to tea started in England, but that is not actually the case. Whatever the case, milk tea has become the symbol of democratic values and resistance against Chinese hegemony. This pan-Asian movement originated in Taiwan and Thailand. The repression by the military dictatorship in Myanmar strengthened the movement, which spread throughout the rest of Asia. The Milk Tea Alliance has no leaders, in stark contrast to China's pyramidal organisation decried by Generation Z, the generation of people born between 1997 and 2010, so digital natives having been brought up in the digital world of the social networks.

This generation dreams of human rights and democracy, cannot abide the Chinese model and will not sacrifice its aspirations on the altar of the economy. For them, economic development cannot be at the expense of democratic values. China, having supported the repression in Myanmar and Hong Kong, stands accused. Its model and expansion are being opposed.

In this context, China actually feels more threatened by the Biden presidency than by the Trump presidency, as Joe Biden's discourse is more centred on human rights and universal values than his predecessor. Shanthi Kalathil, who was the senior director of the International Forum for Democratic Studies at the National Endowment for Democracy, was appointed Deputy Assistant to the President and Coordinator for Democracy and Human Rights at the National Security Council (one of three new coordinator posts created by the White House, along with those for the Middle East and Asia). It should be emphasised that Joe Biden's huge advantage over Donald Trump is internal and external coordination. President Biden travels with his cabinet members, most of whom are far more competent than those of the previous administration. Before the first meeting with China, he took care to organise a meeting with US allies in Asia. He also toured Japan and South Korea.

The first meeting between China and the United States after Joe Biden took office was held on 18 and 19 March 2021 in Anchorage, Alaska. The frigid temperatures and remoteness of the location perhaps say something about the frosty nature of relations between the two powers. The US delegation was led by Secretary of State Antony Blinken and National Security Advisor Jake Sullivan, the Chinese delegation by Director of the Office of the Central Foreign Affairs Commission Yang Jiechi and Minister of Foreign Affairs Wang Yi. Against all expectations, as the Chinese delegation was a guest of the United States, Antony Blinken opened the summit with a two-minute tirade, which elicited an even sharper response from Yang Jiechi that lasted sixteen minutes. The Secretary of State accused China of interference, notably cyberattacks on the United States, and alluded to human rights violations, saying that all these actions "threaten the rules-based order that maintains global stability."[4] Yang Jiechi levelled the same criticisms at the United States. Each accused the other of judging others but not looking at themselves first.

Yang Jiechi's opening remarks, full of certainty, show that China perceives the United States as a declining power, but at the same time feels threatened by the democratic aspirations of young Asians and the rallying of US allies by President Biden, who seems less inclined to haggle over the defence of human rights than his predecessors. At this first meeting with the Biden administration, China spoke as an equal of the United States. The Cold War is now taking place openly, on the world stage, not just behind the scenes.

---

[4] US State Department transcript of the opening remarks at the US–China meeting in Anchorage, Alaska, on Thursday 18 March 2021. https://asia.nikkei.com/Politics/International-relations/US-China-tensions/How-it-happened-Transcript-of-the-US-China-opening-remarks-in-Alaska.

Chapter 14

Loosening the Regulatory Brakes

Businesses are emerging from the COVID-19 crisis laden with debt. Having in general sought to support businesses, governments are even more indebted than before. Admittedly, in countries with highly developed social protection systems, net household savings have increased. This is particularly the case in France. So, how can we re-channel these accumulated savings into projects that will drive the recovery? This is the historic and ongoing role of the banks.

However, to perform their role, banks must have the necessary legal leeway, bearing in mind that banking is a highly regulated industry. As pointed out, regulations were crucial in restoring confidence in the financial system by addressing the excesses that led to the subprime crisis. They constitute a framework to which banks must adhere. But, regulations are like fortifications: they are built on the experience of the most recent crises, not those to come, about which little is known. Cast your mind back to the Maginot Line. A symbol of the superiority of French engineering and warcraft, it was built to withstand an offensive like the one at the start of the First World War. It was undoubtedly very well designed to withstand an attack of this type, although there was no opportunity to verify this, but two decades later proved utterly useless when faced with an adversary not behaving to plan. In many respects, current banking regulations present the same weaknesses.

Recent regulations have focused on strengthening the banks' capital base to enable them to withstand unexpected losses, which is commendable. A considerable proportion of profits generated by banks have thus been taken to reserves, leading to a significant build-up over the last decade.

During the health crisis, the instinct of regulators in the leading jurisdictions was to ramp up these forced savings further: regulators called on banks to refrain from or limit dividends, directing them to transfer profits to reserve. Unable to remunerate their shareholders, or even their members in the case of cooperative banks, banks are now seriously hampered when seeking to go to the market to tap what are abundant savings, bringing into play the multiplier effect that is the hallmark of credit institutions, and thus financing the recovery.

Own funds available to banks, which have been strengthened over the past decade, must cover loans, with the application of a higher percentage the greater the risk. Banking supervisors are constantly revising these percentages upwards. Obsessed as they are by the risk of a bank failure, fearful that lax supervision could be blamed, authorities immediately lock up any excess capital as a preventive measure to deal with any contingency, thereby preventing these funds from being used to grant new loans. Sometimes believing they know better than banks the value of loan portfolios, and in any case, wanting to avert any bank failures, supervisors are hampering the recovery. Longer term, this can be expected to weaken both the banks and the economy.

Having played a central role in the subprime crisis, due to the excesses of certain players lured by the prospect of immediate gains and not sufficiently concerned with the long-term effects of their decisions, but also due to the intervention in the markets of incompetent and poorly supervised investors, the capital markets have been the subject of numerous regulations. These have been aimed at improving the functioning of these markets and limiting opportunities for excessively rapid gains. Entire market segments came to a near standstill and have failed to pick up, securitisation being a case in point. And yet, these activities do play a useful role in the circulation of savings between high-net-worth individuals (increasingly located in Asia) and businesses needing to finance recovery plans (located in Europe or the United States). The case of Europe is particularly disheartening: in parallel with the banking union announced by Nicolas Sarkozy in his Toulon speech and now largely in place, a capital markets union was planned, also intended to improve the efficiency and strength of the euro area. Unfortunately, national interests combined to slow down this splendid project, which is seriously bogged down and perhaps in danger of being shelved. Until then, it is the American and Asian capital markets that will be used, to the delight of the big firms in these countries.

The phenomenon that has plagued the establishment of the capital markets union is symptomatic of the difficulties encountered by major European projects. Besides what is negotiated at the European level, in this case regarding regulations, there is input at the national level. As each member state is different in its psychology, if not its economic reality, it will contribute its own ideas. When it comes to regulations, there is always a reluctance to relax constraints. Each new idea is therefore added to the previous ones. A pile-up is inevitable, all the more so as the supervisors are left to arbitrate. Bear in mind that their interest, indeed their mandate, is to be as strict as possible. They will quickly compare the new ideas from each member state, highlighting what will first be called good practices, then transformed into a guideline, first recommended, and then imposed *de facto* or de jure. While this is going on, the political powers that could stop this proliferation of regulations — the European Council, Commission and Parliament — attend to less technical issues in the public glare, satisfied that they have avoided a repeat of the last crisis, but unaware that, because of their actions, the mechanisms needed now have seized up.

One final example of how applicable regulations are out of sync with the current situation and how EU construction has led to an unnecessary complexity is provided by mechanisms for the recovery and resolution of credit institutions. The two terms refer to two possible situations to which banks may be confronted. Recovery corresponds to a stressed or crisis situation in which a bank's capacity to operate normally is at risk, typically identified when there is a deterioration in its financial performances and one of the recovery indicators defined by regulators is breached. When this happens, the bank must take measures to restore its financial position in accordance with a predefined recovery plan, which must be submitted to the competent authority for review, and whose implementation by management will be closely monitored by this authority. Resolution is the next phase, which for a normal business would lead to insolvency proceedings, but given the importance of banks for the economy in general justifies derogating from ordinary law. The management body and senior management of the bank under resolution are replaced and a predefined, pre-approved resolution plan is implemented by the ad hoc authority. In addition to the fact that the resolution is administered at two levels, national and European, this mechanism means a plan must be drawn up in advance covering recovery and resolution, as a result of a situation that is by definition unknown. The exercise reaches its limits when considering banks that are financially very solid and have a preponderant market share in their country: obviously, such banks could only find themselves in a situation of recovery or resolution if there were dire events, likely to have a cataclysmic effect on the country in which they operate. When considering what scenario might drive Crédit Agricole or Crédit Mutuel to such extremes, it would have to be a default by the French State or a war destroying much of the country. Writing down in advance what actions would need to be taken, in what order and with what financial impact, is an exercise requiring the wildest imagination, for the resolution plan is unlikely ever to be of the slightest usefulness. Yet, hundreds of staff toil on resolution plans in administrations across the euro area and many times that number at Europe's leading commercial banks. They display remarkable intellectual efforts, but their usefulness in the event of a fatal crisis is uncertain, and their contribution to the economic recovery is negative, as with any resource that is misused.

It is quite clear, and quite logical given how laws and regulations are usually created in response to serious events and therefore ex post, that the current regulations unnecessarily restrict the banks' ability to finance the economic recovery post-pandemic. Since the supervisors' task is enforcing compliance with regulations, and the regulators' task is writing these regulations, not repealing them, it will be left to the executive arm to take back control and drive the necessary changes. This effort must naturally be at both the European and national levels.

In light of the specific instances of regulatory overkill cited previously, one of the first priorities must be to put a stop to the constant increase in the banks' capital requirements. Past a certain threshold, which is already defined in international regulations through leverage ratios, banks should regain full control of their future profits. They must be able to self-finance their growth, contribute to financing the economic recovery and remunerate their shareholders. Banks need to maintain access to the stock market, with shareholders, rather than the state, absorbing losses in the event of a crisis, in return for what, in normal times, should be an attractive remuneration.

If the first priority is to enable banks to lend again on a massive scale, the second must be to unblock European capital markets, which have been held back by the complexities surrounding the capital markets union project. On this highly technical subject, a working group bringing together financial intermediaries, businesses and investors could easily come up with a few immediate measures to harness the euro capital market and have it drive Europe's economic recovery. Let's not be naive: let's invite only European players to the table if we don't want, as in the past, to leave the field to American or, now, British players.

We could also address what is clearly a level of sophistication out of all proportion to its potential usefulness, by reducing the level of detail and frequency of the review of recovery and resolution plans, at least for the most solid banks. This would save the salaries of several hundred government and EU officials. This would also free up the technical skills of some of the banking industry's best specialists who unnecessarily devote their time to a task of theoretical interest.

Chapter 15

Smarter Regulations

To prevent regulations, in this case for banks, from becoming so many Maginot Lines, they need to be fit for purpose and so have the desired outcome during future crises, the timing and nature of which are unknown. The difficulty of the task leads to reactions of two types.

One type might be called peremptory regulations. Deriving from the discretionary power of the issuer, new regulations are imposed relying precisely on the powers that go with the office, often intentionally drawing a very large amount of public attention. Uncertainty as to their subsequent applicability is brushed aside by the force of the announcement. Cast your mind back to Donald Trump summoning the entire media circus to make a martial announcement and sign presidential decrees with a big black marker. Playing to the audience might cover the murmurs of doubt, but the reality of the situation is stubborn and does not always bend to presidential injunctions. When they do not fall foul of the judiciary for being poorly conceived, as was frequently the case in the United States, measures of this type are rarely very effective. It has to be said that the art of being a banker, based on striking the right balance between risk-taking and the profitability needed to remain a going concern, does not lend itself well to off-the-cuff regulations.

The other temptation, in France at least, has been to entrust the drafting of regulations to the specialists, to the brilliant and dedicated technocrats that are the country's pride. It is left to them, the "wisest of the wise", to draft with precision and subtlety the details of the regulations. The recommendations issued by France's High Council for Financial Stability are a good example. Fearing that banks would loosen lending standards for housing loans, France's macroprudential authority stepped in, defining what it felt were the right lending criteria. It blissfully ignored the banks' long experience in this matter and knowledge of their customers, as borne out by their track record over the economic cycles. It imposed very precise restrictions, notably a benchmark ceiling for the debt service-to-income (DSTI) ratio of 35%, with the possibility of diverging from this within certain limits: "part of the volume of total loans may diverge from best practices. This flexibility margin must be strictly proportionate and be able to be justified by reference to a written policy. The flexibility margin for the share of new loans may diverge from best practices by up to 20% of the quarterly volume of total new loans (excluding renegotiations, loan buybacks and credit consolidation). At least 80% of the flexibility margin must be reserved for the purchase of the main residence and at least 30% of the flexibility margin must be specifically reserved for first-time buyers."[1] This could not be more precise, but the scruples of technocrats led them to add the following: "The High Council will monitor the risk profile of loans granted under the flexibility margin, particularly with regard to the borrowers' debt levels."[2]

For once, no need to look to Brussels to find a text that is too convoluted to be understood by its intended recipients (lenders and borrowers) or integrated into the banks' information systems. Well intentioned, and drafted after weeks of consultation with various experts, this type of regulation gives the appearance of seriousness but never produces the desired effect.

To be followed, any regulation must be understood and integrated by the person to whom it applies. The person must understand its essential purpose and have in mind its main elements.

Consider the recommendations issued by France's High Council for Financial Stability. How can you explain to someone earning €10,000 a month that, because of the 35% ceiling for the DSTI ratio, the bank cannot extend a loan that would result in monthly instalments of more than €3,500, leaving the person with €6,500 a month for living expenses, when someone earning €2,000 a month, paying back a loan in monthly instalments of €700, will be expected to live on €1,300 a month? Even though the bank and the customer may agree that €3,000 would be ample to cover

---

[1] https://www.economie.gouv.fr/files/2021-01/Recommandation_R-HCSF-2021-1.pdf?v=1625159339.

[2] *Ibid.*

living expenses, which would leave €7,000 to cover monthly loan instalments, it will be a case of "no can do" because the authorities have so decided. A parallel can be drawn with the famous 80 km/h speed limit introduced by the French government that so angered the population and caused months of disorder. The desire to regulate down to the smallest detail produces rejection or ignorance. Paraphrasing Louis Dembitz Brandeis, who served as an associate justice on the Supreme Court of the United States, if we desire respect for regulations, we must first make regulations respectable.

This begs the question as to why regulations are imposed in the first place. In principle, compliance is not an end in itself. Regulations seek to organise the behaviour of members of a profession harmoniously, avoid the most common dangers and protect consumers from the sometimes deviant practices of certain members. In short, they have a purpose that everyone can understand and for which there is consensus. Elected representatives, acting for the people, must then pass laws that no one is supposed to ignore. Banking regulations do not proceed from such an idyllic vision.

Yet, there is nothing utopian about this. There are regulations known and understood by the public at large and generally all the more respected for being less abstruse. The Highway Code is a good example, the unfortunate episode of the 80 km/h speed limit in France coming as a timely reminder. Although greatly added to since its first versions in the 19th century, it remains a readable document: the articles are short, the jargon is not excessive. Since it is comprehensible and meets a simple need (to avoid accidents), no one disputes it, even though it is not followed strictly by everyone.

Regulations can impose constraints on individual behaviour: the Highway Code prohibits driving under the influence of alcohol or drugs; banking regulations prohibit paying excessive bonuses to market traders. In both cases, individual freedom is restricted in the name of the general interest. In a democracy, this constraint is accepted. For the rest, it should be a case of "everything which is not forbidden is allowed", as the legal maxim goes.

Regulations, whether it is the Highway Code or the Monetary and Financial Code, spell out how to behave, or more precisely how not to behave. What they don't say, and should not try to say, is what action to take. You don't consult the Highway Code to know where to go; driving a car is not simply about following the signs on the side of the road, and you would be mad to behave like that. You decide where you are going, the Highway Code sets certain constraints on how to get there. You have to think of banking regulations in the same way: their purpose is not to dictate a specific policy to the banks, or at least they should not have that objective, for this amounts to interference and *de facto* management, but they can lay down rules that you have to respect when pursuing a particular strategy.

Too many bankers around the world have complained that their strategy or lending policy was being defined by the supervisory authorities for us not to try to understand what has prompted such disillusionment. It is certainly tempting for the powers that be in France to encourage banks to lend to some rather than others, in support of one policy or another: defend French agriculture, encourage economic development in deprived areas, promote environmentally responsible industries, etc. But, in a world of freedom, where banks are no longer state owned, the only justification for a regulation is to avoid accidents and keep the traffic moving.

If some regulations appear so complex, it is because they sometimes have hidden, not to say illegitimate, objectives. Political objectives are legitimate when passing laws, but have no place in detailed technical rules for a particular sector, even one as central as banking. Banking regulations would be clearer, banks would be more efficient if politics were kept out of the mix.

For at least five decades now, managers all the way to the boardroom have been told that to lead their staff, they have to give them a sense of purpose, set broad objectives and give them some autonomy, proportionate to the team's experience. The results speak for themselves: between the liberal, or even liberated, enterprise and the kolkhoz, one system works well and the other badly. So, why shouldn't the regulation of banks, at least those having a long track record and having demonstrated their professionalism, follow the same principle? The reality is quite otherwise, as current regulations are infantilising. Clearly, this situation will have less positive outcomes. More importantly, it will not allow banks to adapt to changing circumstances. Like any centralised and standardised system, it contains the seeds of sclerosis, the premise being that regulated sectors of activity lack all intelligence. It is the worst recipe in times of change.

Chapter 16

Financing the New Environmental Cycle

There is a common thread linking the COVID-19 crisis and the climate crisis, which, for some, is under way, while for others it simply looms on the horizon. What they have in common is their global nature. No individual, no company, no human category and no state can overcome the virus or the slow warming of the atmosphere alone, because whatever they do, the behaviour of others will have a much greater impact than their own. One of the consequences of this reality is the reluctance to act first because of the sense that this would be pointless. And indeed, individual action doesn't help much in itself, but it can set an example that gradually leads to collective action, which alone can succeed.

The second thing these two crises — viral pandemic and global warming — have in common is that there are enough scientists to say anything and everything about the situation and the remedies. This does not make it any easier for political leaders to take decisions, already being little motivated by the global dimension of the problem, which logically reduces their capacity to influence the outcome.

And yet, everyone knows it in their bones, it is in our common interest to act, for we are wasting the planet's resources and transforming these resources into greenhouse gases and other toxic by-products, when we first need to slow the increase in emissions and then reduce them. We all need to act not only to the best of our personal ability but also in conjunction with others and according to common principles. But, what are we to do without a universal conductor to direct our response? Even the superpowers, the United States and China, cannot stop global warming on their own. We need a United Nations, but the one we've had for three-quarters of a century doesn't have the necessary authority. Or maybe a divine intervention, but what we have are competing religions, whose followers seek not universalism but confrontation. Will a universal conscience emerge? Some believe that social networks could be the catalyst. We hope so, but do not expect this spontaneous movement to be some kind of magical solution.

Under these conditions, more modestly and realistically, one could imagine each state encouraging citizens to act within its space. Governments could do this out of virtue, aware of the need for everyone to act even when there is no conductor to orchestrate the world's response, or out of necessity, eager to address the concerns of those citizens expecting action on this front, particularly in democracies where the voice of the people does count. As for despots, who all claim to be enlightened, they will no doubt follow out of pride if all the countries, in particular their allies, go down this road. However, one difficulty remains: any remedial action is going to be expensive, far more than can be afforded by countries, which are laden with debt after years when borrowing came easy and now a pandemic that required the mobilisation of colossal financial resources. This is where banks could step into the breach.

What, broadly speaking, do we need to do to reverse the potentially deadly trend we are on? Without going into the details, for everyone has their own solutions, convictions or obsessions, what needs to change is the amount of energy consumed and the way it is produced. Climate disruption will first and foremost disrupt established patterns for all aspects of energy.

Consuming less energy means living a little differently, but no less well. For example, recycling what is no longer needed or designing each new product to be more economical to manufacture and use than its predecessor. Some industries have been pushed in this direction, usually by regulations, such as the automotive industry, which has achieved targets for vehicle fuel consumption that were unimaginable just a few years ago, with the industry now moving towards full electrification.

Producing our energy in a way that is more respectful of resources means calling into question the massive use of hydrocarbons, which we know are finite resources. The day will come when these resources run out, probably in the not-too-distant future at the current rate, a day that our children will see if we do nothing. It would not be too much of an effort, for short distance trips, to wheel out your bike instead of riding a scooter or driving a car.

Electricity can be produced using renewable resources, such as solar or wind power, and this will soon cost less than electricity produced using fossil fuels. What will be expensive is dismantling existing thermal power stations and erecting solar farms or wind farms, terms that are so much more bucolic than the term plant or station with its industrial connotations. What is going to be expensive is not the energy produced more sustainably in the future, but the energy transition. This will entail taking money where it is stashed, namely, in the banks.

The timing could not be better because, as pointed out, banks are where households have put their savings, and these have never been so plentiful in rich countries, for the rich have emerged richer from the crisis, as always. Banks can transform these savings to finance major energy transition projects. To do this, it is not enough for these projects to be guided in the direction desired by governments; they must also be of sufficient economic interest for the banks. Services provided by bank need to be fairly remunerated, for they are economic agents operating in a competitive world and accountable to their shareholders. There are two possible ways of going about this, both of which are in the hands of governments: pump priming and taxation.

With pump priming, the states would contribute a small part of the financing, assuming first any eventual losses. While this would only cover a small part of the sums needed, the capital provided in this way would pay a crucial role, being what is known as catalytic first-loss capital, but would attract a disproportionate capital charge under current regulations if provided by the banks. States, not being subject to the same rules, can use fairly modest sums in this way, which would have a multiplier effect through the amount of the loans that can then be extended by the banks. This was the mechanism used very astutely by the French government with the state-backed Recovery participating loans (prêts participatifs Relance — PPR).

Taxation, another weapon available to governments, can be used to favour renewable energy over thermal energy. There is plenty of scope for this, as energy in its varied forms is heavily taxed in every country. In France, taxes account for around 60% of the price of petrol and 40% of the price of electricity. By changing the level of taxation applied to energy consumed according to its origin, renewable or not, and without changing the total amount collected by the states so as to not weigh on public finances or on taxpayers, the production of renewable energy can become sufficiently profitable to pay off bank loans taken out to finance investment in wind farms and solar farms, indeed any other source of renewable energy that might be developed in the future thanks to human ingenuity.

The banks would find in this an economically profitable application of their resources, which, it should be remembered, are currently placed for a significant part with central banks. In Europe, far from remunerating these deposits, central banks charge what amounts to a custody fee in the form of negative real interest rates. This type of lending by banks would also be consistent with individual objectives in term of green financing. For some years now, shareholders and creditors, and soon European regulations, have urged banks to channel their lending into financing energy transition projects.

Alongside these investments in new energy sources, energy consumption must be cut. While investments are a matter for governments to steer in line with an ecological policy that is never more than a revamped industrial policy, and for businesses to implement and turn a profit, consumption is everyone's concern, and first and foremost for individuals. Here too, taxation and actions by commercial banks can be harnessed to rapid effect at no cost to governments.

Going back to the example of the automotive industry, which in less than half a decade has gone from being a symbol of freedom to being a scapegoat for pollution, the bonus–malus systems put in place in France mean that, at zero cost to the public purse, certain goods (electric vehicles) can be favoured to the detriment of others (gas-guzzlers). The same could be said for a host of other energy-intensive goods, from boilers to light bulbs, household appliances, building materials and smartphones depending on energy consumed during production and operation, agricultural products depending on whether obtained from natural farming or factory farming, clothing that may or may not include recycling efforts, etc. Depending on the case, a specific system or simply the introduction of ad quantum or differentiated VAT rates would encourage the consumption of more environmentally friendly products.

Credits extended by banks to finance consumption, particularly purchases of vehicles, furniture or electronics, could also be used as an incentive to promote ecologically responsible consumption. There are two ways in which this could be regulated: tax advantages (households could deduct the interest paid to finance the purchase of eligible goods from their taxable income) or regulatory incentives (a loan taken out to finance the purchase of an eligible good would entitle the bank to apply a reduced capital charge).

Chapter 17

Financing Building Renovation

When it comes to basic needs, prominence has always been given to shelter for giving protection against the elements. No material good possesses the usefulness or is as emotionally charged as the home, acting as a sanctuary, a place of human closeness for family members and friends. What's more, for the immense majority, the acquisition of the family home will surpass all other heads of expenditure. So it is no surprise that for many men and women across the generations, having a home of their own has been an enduring dream. For most, their mortgage will be the biggest debt they take on in their lives. And for many banks, mortgages occupy an essential and sometimes dominant place on their balance sheet.

In France, residential mortgage loans represent €1,143 billion, or 84% of bank loans and advances to households. Of course, banks also lend to businesses, to the tune of €1,202 billion, of which €310 billion is directly linked to commercial real estate. All in all, 57% of bank loans to households and businesses directly finance real estate. Each month, €15 billion to €20 billion of new loans are granted in France for the acquisition of new or existing properties. What can be done for all this money to contribute to reducing energy consumption?

It is a question worth exploring. All estimates show that housing is a major source of energy loss: in France, the building sector alone (so not taking into account construction) accounts for 45% of energy consumption and 27% of greenhouse gas emissions. France introduced the requirement for an energy performance diagnosis (diagnostic de performance énergétique — DPE) in 2006, since when there have been efforts to improve its reliability. All sellers and landlords must now include this diagnosis in the technical diagnosis file (dossier de diagnostic technique — DDT) provided to buyers or tenants. Energy performance diagnoses have identified 4.8 million homes as being poorly insulated (i.e. classified as F or G, the two lowest levels of the seven rating classes). According to the French Ministry for Ecological Transition, there are 7 million poorly insulated homes in France or 14% of the housing stock. A bill, arising from the work of the Citizens' Convention on Climate, calls for a ban on the letting of all these properties from 2028 (already, since 1 January 2023, a dwelling can be let only if final energy consumption is less than 450 kWh per square metre per year, determined by reference to the net living area). It would seem reasonable to expect that sooner or later there will be a ban on the sale of these properties, which is already the case for properties not connected to an individual or collective wastewater disposal system. Clearly, measures of this type are a very strong incentive to renovate substandard properties.

Another strong incentive, for current occupants as well as future buyers and tenants, is that, after carrying out thermal insulation work, annual heating costs can be cut by around €1,000 for a previously poorly insulated property. All or part of these annual savings could be spent on energy renovation without putting a strain on anyone's finances. As for the state, in collaboration with local authorities, it plans to invest €4.8 billion over five years to insulate public buildings. It also intends to provide €1.2 billion in aid to low-income households and €3 billion in subsidised loans to social landlords. In total, the state would provide €9 billion in aid and loans over five years, which is not to be sniffed at, but bear in mind that it barely represents property loans granted by banks in a fortnight. Government departments have alluded to this firepower here and there in their communication, but that's about it. This resource is not for them to channel as they please, but they can influence the outcome. Not only is it 120 times more than what the government has budgeted, but it would come at no cost to the taxpayer.

Channelling this recurring source of financing such as to encourage a reduction in energy consumption, in particular through the elimination of poorly insulated homes, will have to draw on two levers: as these are loans agreed between banks and homeowners, the homeowner must find the arrangement to be in his financial interest, while the bank will want the loan to fit into its financial model.

As to the first condition, the owners of the premises must be convinced that the work will be a source of savings, i.e. reduce energy consumption and therefore energy bills. With annual savings put at €1,000 on average, an around €9,500 loan could be arranged, at what are currently very low interest rates. That's a very simple way of incentivising homeowners, as they can be sure of seeing the value of their property appreciate. For poorly insulated properties, carrying out the work may be the only way to find a buyer or a tenant.

As to the second, it is possible to incentivise banks to grant this type of loan, referred to as "self-liquidating" in the financial jargon because the resulting savings for the borrower will of themselves enable the loan to be repaid, even in the case of a low-income individual presenting, on the face of things, a greater risk. That can be accomplished simply enough by having these loans benefit from a state guarantee fund, which would come at a minimal cost given the very low default rates for residential mortgage loans in France, or giving the bank a right to reimbursement in the event of the subsequent sale of the property by the owner. It would be possible to apply the funds lying dormant to home savings schemes (plans d'épargne logement — PEL) for existing properties, which give access to subsidised loans. Banks would likely seize the opportunity and be prepared to charge a zero interest rate, for these resources cost them a pretty penny. With a bit of imagination, a bit of cooperation between the banks and the Finance Ministry as with the state-guaranteed loans (prêts garantis par l'État — PGE) and Recovery participating loans (prêts participatifs Relance — PPR), it is not ten times but a hundred times what is currently budgeted for the thermal renovation of buildings that could be made available, without any deterioration in the banks' risk exposure or affecting the solvency of households.

There is a significant need, for the work required is estimated at €148 billion over ten years. This sum would be well within the banks' means if they see financial benefits are to be had. Time is of the essence, however, since this will require accompanying measures: changes to taxation, standardisation of energy requirements, revision to the uses to which savings plans can be put, etc. Also, apart from its effect on global warming, this type of action would stimulate activity and employment in the building sector, giving work to members of the building trade right across the country.

Chapter 18

Beyond Our Borders

It is a fairly common character trait that everyone will insist, like the Americans, "this is my country, grandest on earth." Most in France are convinced that their country is a great power, but let's take a closer look.

In days of old, the power of an empire or kingdom was measured by its population. For all men were equal with nothing but the clothes on their back, before education, technical progress, philosophies and policies adopted by one society or another accelerated the progress of some over others. Until then, power was strictly proportional to population, the bigger it was, the more people to tax and send off to war. Based on this criterion, France accounts for just under 1% of the world's population and ranks 22nd.

Another indicator for measuring power, at least if the millions of deaths caused by wars fought over the centuries are anything to go by, is territory, land if you prefer. In bygone days, every peasant, village, empire or kingdom would have attested to that. France, even including its overseas territories and, in particular, the huge expanse of the French Guiana, accounts for only 0.45% of the world's land surface and ranks 41st.

Of course, population and territory alone cannot express a nation's power, though the blood of our ancestors has been spilt for just that. As our concern here is the economy, beyond a mere census or lines on a map, let us consider by what other criteria one might take stock of a country. For this purpose, we have long measured the gross domestic product of each country and, subsequently, that of the world as a whole. On this basis, France accounts for around 3% of world output and ranks 5th or 6th.

Now, these criteria, commonly used for ranking countries in relation to one another, reveal what tends to be overlooked: for all its prestige, France weighs less than 5% in the grand scheme of things, whatever the indicator used. For some nationalists rooted in the past, this factual observation is cause for regret. For those having succumbed to xenophobia, it is a source of paranoia. For those, on the other hand, who want to shape the future, for those who see more "opportunity" (jī, 机) than "danger" (wēi, 危) in the Chinese ideogram for crisis, for those who climb to the top of the mountain that encloses their valley or the mast that carries the ship's sails to scan the horizon, there is something to enthuse about in the observation of the world's immensity.

There will be those who join in the lamentations, to which we would oppose a less blinkered vision. To those complaining that nothing is possible in France, well there is 99.6% of the world's land surface where such strictures do not apply, where surely their (ill-founded) whining would be without cause. To those who believe nothing more can be sold to French consumers, there are one hundred more customers the world over. To those who measures growth to France's borders but not beyond, one might point out that 97% of the world economy moves to a different beat, which is often more vivacious.

As regards the economic recovery post-COVID, this opening to the world is cause for some optimism, revealing a growth path.

Don't lose sight of another factor, which is that economies in different countries depend in part on national political decisions, local education and health systems, and bodies of laws and regulations that differ from one place to another — tax law, labour law, competition law, etc. There is therefore a diversification effect, with companies with international operations always seeing some geographical markets doing better than others, smoothing out business performances. The same has obviously been true of the current pandemic, the health effects of which have manifested themselves at different times in different countries, with highly contrasting health and economic consequences depending on government choices and resources. The forced closure of supposedly non-essential shops in France occurred when consumption in China was growing strongly.

One cannot therefore recommend enough to national champions, in France as elsewhere, especially those whose products are attractive enough to have already convinced local consumers, to look at the big picture. There are billions of foreign consumers, sometimes just across the border, sometimes on the other side of the world: some will be very different but, sometimes, and increasingly so, they will in fact have very similar lifestyles.

Such an undertaking is obviously not for the faint-hearted. An ambitious vision is required of the chief executive from the word go, but then you do not get to climb the corporate pyramid and stay at the apex for any length of time without being ambitious. It takes a dose of courage too, a willingness to bet on the future and an entrepreneurial spirit. It also takes resources and, especially, the help of others to embark on a new path towards unknown customers. Of course, national champions can build on an existing product offering and already enjoy brand recognition.

French businesses enjoy a considerable advantage, envied by many countries, which is the "Made in France" label. Through the ages and different political systems (monarchy, revolution, republic), France's leaders have always endeavoured to showcase the excellence of their country, with which they obviously identified. Chambord, Fontainebleau and Versailles bear witness to this in the field of architecture. For centuries, France's art of living and intellectual culture have been held up as examples of perfection the word over, mocked on occasions, but widely recognised for what they are. French presidents have nurtured this image by hosting visiting foreign dignitaries at these prestigious venues. For several years now, the French government has been promoting this image, renaming some entities with high profiles abroad to incorporate the country's name (France Stratégie, Business France, France Digitale, Team France Export, etc.), establishing a marketing framework for French companies. The "Made in France" label opens doors, providing French companies with a competitive advantage. Businesses are not always aware of the emotional charge that a product labelled "Made in France" can have on consumers on the other side of the world.

Serving this international ambition is another area where banks have a role to play. France has powerful banks, as pointed out, and these have been present in leading economies for a very long time. Lest it be forgotten, in 1900, Crédit Lyonnais overtook its rivals to become the world's largest bank by total assets. Provincial though it was, Crédit Lyonnais opened a branch in London in 1870, as Paris was under siege and carried business from there rather than Paris. Branches were opened in St Petersburg and Odessa in the time of the Tsars, in Alexandria and Constantinople in the time of the Sultans. Almost all of France's leading commercial banks were founded between the end of the Second Empire and the beginning of the Third Republic, going on to participate in the international development of French industrialists and merchants, from the Russian railway projects at the end of the 19th century to sales of the Rafale aircraft at the beginning of the 21st century. Networks have been developed on every continent and they have recognised expertise in the traditions and customs of international trade. Some, such as the Banque Française du Commerce Extérieur,[1] which was established in the aftermath of the Second World War, were intended solely to support France's international development by facilitating cooperation between major public and private players, in the name of the industrial policy of the time. Almost all of them have a department or subsidiary dedicated to providing financial and operational support to customers exporting or setting up business outside France. Depending on the size of the company and the bank's commercial policy, services provided to French companies abroad will be through a local subsidiary of the French bank, or by a local bank with which it has a bank agency agreement.

In the service of this international ambition, the state has a role to play by backing the private sector's efforts. One notable initiative in the French government's recovery plan is the inclusion of measures to develop exports, framed with the help of foreign trade advisers[2] selected from the business community to ensure that these measures would be practical and would produce significant effects with a limited outlay of funds. While the sum devoted remains modest (€250 million in a total recovery plan of €100 billion, which is inevitably very domestic), the measures are concrete: export guarantee and pre-financing, prospecting insurance covering costs in the event of failure, insurance for short-term export credits in the event a foreign buyer defaults, subsidies for the hiring of young French graduates under the Volunteering for International Experience (VIE) programme to support export projects on the ground, access to free information on foreign markets, etc. All these measures are designed to have both a psychological impact (reassuring first-time exporters so that they can make a move) and a very practical one (providing information, covering the cost of an initial setback).

---

[1] Acquired by Crédit National in 1996, the two entities going on to merge to form Natixis.
[2] Foreign Trade Advisors (Conseillers du Commerce extérieur — CCE) are appointed by decree from the Prime Minister. They are chosen notably from among corporate officers, executive managers and independent professionals for having recognised expertise in the field of international economic relations.

The French government's €100 billion Relance recovery plan focuses resources mainly on the energy transition and the competitiveness of the country's enterprises. Of this, €40 billion is being provided by the European Union. To kick-start the economic recovery, the European Union has established a temporary instrument, NextGenerationEU (NGEU), which has been endowed with €750 billion. The amount is impressive in itself, even more so the financing: for the first time, the European Commission borrowed funds on behalf of the European Union with the approval of the member states, all ratifying the Own Resources Decision (ORD). The community of destinies having found expression in the single market now extends to the financing of the European Union. One does not always appreciate the effort this represents for the German people, the only truly thrifty people in the Union, the only people to have experienced bankruptcy leading to the physical destruction of their country, and naturally the most reluctant to co-sign a bond issue with Latin neighbours considered to be inveterate spendthrifts. When you are the strongest, but seek strength in numbers, you are bound to turn to someone weaker than you are. Easy to say, harder to do, and above all harder to get your voters to understand.

After governments wrapped up negotiations to define this unprecedented plan, a year passed before the ORD secured approval by all EU member states according to their constitutional requirements. This delay was a sign of the reluctance of the people's elected representatives to abdicate part of their sovereignty in this way — a matter of financial sovereignty for some, nationalism for others. This often lengthy process of public decision-making, especially in democratic systems, is in stark contrast to the agility that businesses advocate as a management style, and which many demonstrated during the pandemic. But, when the institutions take on the mantle of a superpower, which only the European Union can claim on a par with the United States and China, and when it serves as a support or catalyst for private initiatives, then its effect is massive. That's why this recovery plan is historic, and why it has the potential to change the world we live in.

Conclusion

A new world or "the same, only a little worse"?[1]

The current crisis raises many questions. We have looked to past crises for similarities, and have found some. They point to the dangers that lie ahead once the epidemic is behind us. Exacerbated nationalism, deepening inequalities, a frenzy of redundant projects — long is the list of pitfalls that accompany a crisis exit, but none are new. If we finally regain the clear-sightedness we so lacked in the face of the coronavirus, we will be able to identify pitfalls and avoid them.

But, this crisis, as we have shown, is very different from those experienced in the past. To use Michel Houellebecq's comparison, it perhaps bears the most similarities to the plagues of the Middle Ages. Should we therefore lament a lost millennium or try the remedies of the Renaissance? We don't think so, because the current crisis is also showing us the way out. An unprecedented way out of a crisis that is no less unprecedented: the promise of a new world that is neither the same nor worse than the world before. In our areas of expertise, economics and finance, we discern the broad outlines of this path.

Let us first take stock. A crisis is the eruption of a phenomenon that was not anticipated. It takes almost everyone by surprise. In this respect, the health crisis was the perfect storm. There followed a period of stupefaction, which this time was fairly long, and then a process of trial and

---

[1] www.francetvinfo.fr/sante/maladie/coronavirus/coronavirus-pourmichel-houellebecq-le-monde-d-apres-sera-le-meme-en-un-peupire_3948117.html.

error in coming up with ad hoc solutions not envisaged beforehand. In this free-for-all of ideas, where the best rubs elbows with the worst, certain ideas previously ruled out as utopian can emerge as suddenly credible solutions. This is what has just happened.

The most obvious example, which goes well beyond financial phenomena, is remote working. Not so long ago, trade unions and employees were clamouring to be allowed to work from home part of the time. Employers often suspected this was a pretext for sleeping in instead of attending morning meetings. Almost always, they argued that this was physically impossible. Then came widespread lockdowns in France and many other developed countries. To the general surprise of employees and employers alike, remote working became the new norm for many businesses, enabling the performance of most tasks without employees leaving the house except to buy essential supplies or obtain medical care. While there is widespread recognition that this working arrangement also has its disadvantages, particularly for creating group dynamics or brainstorming, no one is seriously considering returning to previous practices. In France, remote working was the rare privilege of a few employees, mostly women, who had fought hard to obtain the right to work from home one day a week. The future of work is hybrid, with some time spent at the employer's premises and some time spent working elsewhere. Technology has made this technically possible, while lockdowns have shown that it was financially viable and socially acceptable. Hybrid working is financially viable in that, for employers, it can lead to a reduction in fixed occupancy costs by downsizing office buildings. It is socially acceptable, having been embraced by the entire population, to the point that entire sections of France's Labour Code will probably have to be rewritten, as some already outdated provisions were definitively shelved in 2020.

Task sharing within a team structure, such as document co-authoring, can be performed remotely, as all you need is a broadband connection, transport and office space no longer being constraints. Members of staff are just a click away from their managers, and there are ways of guarding against intrusive practices (mute function, message recording). Remote working was a dream. Many tried it out, and it does seem to be in touch with today's generation. In addition to the financial aspects linked to this working arrangement, which can be used extensively, it is becoming a must for recruiting young talent, particularly the most promising, who are often the most demanding. Few businesses will dispense with hybrid working. It is a safe bet that none of the businesses that will be leaders in their industry ten years hence will have opted not to benefit from the advantages procured by remote working.

Another revelation of the pandemic crisis is that banks are in fine shape, able to help their customers overcome temporary difficulties and, at least for most of them, able to absorb an increase in the cost of risk associated with bankruptcies, which may have been pushed back in time but are inevitable. As we have seen, after the Great Recession, it was the financial solidity of banks on which regulators focused. The positive effect of these regulations was not that they averted another subprime crisis — for crises never repeat themselves — but that they ensured banks had adequate capital to tackle the economic fallout of the pandemic. In most countries, governments delved into the state coffers to help businesses, even individuals in those countries where social safety nets are notoriously inadequate, such as the United States. Even so, it is a fact that the banks were the first to systematically offer to defer loan repayments by customers directly affected by the crisis. With branches remaining open during lockdowns, banks stood by their small business customers (shopkeepers, craftsmen, etc.), helping them find the best solutions to their financial difficulties. Of vital importance for these efforts not to be in vain was that no one is better able than banks to determine which businesses, tradesmen and organisations can be expected to overcome their difficulties if there is help to tide them over. Banks have always been, are and always will be in the business of risk management, which cannot be said of states with the same certainty. Banks do no tend to get it wrong: in the past three decades, the average cost of risk for the major banks has been 1% of loans; 99 times out of 100, they get it right and are repaid. This is a parallel source of financing to that of governments, which is all the more attractive given that banks are flush with liquidity and therefore do not need to borrow more. To unleash the banks' energy, all that is needed is to remove unnecessary constraints imposed by regulations.

As with working practices, the more or less strict lockdowns revolutionised consumption. Restricted in their geographical mobility, denied access to stores closed on government orders, or simply afraid of being contaminated, consumers changed their habits. Home deliveries multiplied, from a pizza ordered from the restaurant next door to a flat screen all the way from a Chinese factory. Solidarity towards local shopkeeper and producers manifested itself in "shop local" movements. The result has been a boom at both ends of the spectrum: on the one hand, a surge in demand for local products, whose quality was rediscovered; on the other, a boom in global e-commerce, offering the widest choice at the click of a mouse. These two trends will undoubtedly persist, but will likely fade slightly. The big winners in 2020 were delicatessens and technology-oriented multinationals. In addition to hybrid work, there will also be hybrid consumption, both very local and very global.

Each crisis accentuates pre-existing economic disparities. This health crisis was no exception. But, it has also been accompanied by a new aspiration for a quite different world which, to be built, will require broad consensus (for it involves everyone) and significant investments (for it entails a long, costly transition). It is therefore important, not only from a moral standpoint but also simply for the functioning of the world, that this be accompanied by a better distribution of wealth. Not necessarily that everyone should have the same income, for this has already been tried and has led to disaster by ruining any incentive to innovate, take risks or work harder, but that everyone should have the conviction that their situation will improve at the same rate as the world in which they live, that their children's lives will be better than their own, that the future holds more promises than threats. While building trust is essential, for without the support of the general population there can be no lasting change, more attention must be given to some categories. Long would be the list of these categories, so let's focus on the biggest, namely, women: in many countries, women are poorly paid, if not mistreated, and they undoubtedly remain the human resource that is least recognised and most poorly utilised by our society, even today.

As far as women are concerned, it should be emphasised that economic progress will be that much greater if the gender pay gap is reduced, and also if access to credit were on the same terms as for men. In some countries, banks take great care not to discriminate in this area, but this is not the case in general. Financial inclusion is also an issue with other categories, pretty well anyone not fitting into the neat little boxes defined in the past by the banks (the young, immigrants, social outcasts, etc.). In the future, banks will have to be more inclusive if they are to fulfil their role in society properly and, in so doing, have a lasting place in tomorrow's world.

Faced with all these developments shaping the post-COVID world, we have pointed out the stifling effects of current banking regulations. To overcome these effects, regulations need changing. For once, it is not a question of correcting regulations to prevent there being another crisis, from which we can recover, but to bring about a dramatic transformation of the world. What do we want? Smart regulations, which must be intelligible: in a word, simple.

The induced effect of COVID-19 is that by demonstrating the fragility of our life on earth, the pandemic has reminded some people of the dangers associated with global warming, which slowly but inexorably is putting living species, including our own, in mortal danger. At the same time, by driving many city dwellers into temporary exile in the countryside, lockdowns gave some citizens a real taste of the quality of life that comes with living in surroundings that are less crowded, less polluted, less noisy — in a word, less hostile. So, the world to which many more citizens than before aspire is one that is decarbonised, more respectful of nature, and more economical with resources — in short, green. For many, growth must henceforth be green. The current difficulties have opened the world's eyes to the long-term risks. This can but be welcomed, but it must come with the realisation that more responsible growth, while certainly possible, will demand considerable efforts, particularly in financial terms. It is not so much getting a greener economy to function (with renewable energies, soft mobility, hybrid work and eco-friendly housing) that will be onerous, but transforming our current economy, which is brown or rather greyish, into a green economy in the first place. Just look at the sheer number of motor vehicles to be replaced, the buildings to be insulated, the railways to be maintained to the same standards as motorways, the transition to regenerative agriculture, the transition from waste management to resource efficiency, etc. In each case, it is a matter of financing today what will make our lives better tomorrow. Who can do this and for each economic agent? The banks, better than anyone. It is no coincidence that the banks closest to their customers (for they are also their members or shareholders) and to urban and rural communities (for their networks span these territories) are all preparing to play a major role in the energy transition. This is an opportunity to be seized, not just for banks but for society as a whole.

While ecological issues constitute a collective challenge, it is on a very personal level that individuals perceive threats to their health. Individual reactions to the pandemic demonstrated this intimate, irrational perception of what many call our "most prized possession". As a result, the threats posed by our lifestyles and consumption habits, revealed by the rapid overcrowding of our hospitals and the more or less explicit abandonment of certain patients to their sad fate, are taken more seriously than in the past. As before, solutions will often come at a financial cost if populations are to live in better conditions and grow old outside medical structures intended to treat serious cases. The need for financing, advisory services, financial planning and so on could provide a possible role for bankers in tomorrow's world.

Global warming is a challenge for the entire planet. Pandemics such as the one we have just experienced are a challenge for the whole of humanity. However, concrete actions to meet these challenges are necessarily at the local level. Each house and each car contributes to global warming. Contamination must be prevented in all bars and discotheques, long enough for the entire population to be vaccinated. The measures needed, the incentives to be offered and the initiatives to be encouraged must be local. Industry's weight in the economy has shrunk steadily, but Taylorism may not yet have outlived its usefulness. Human existence is another matter, for it is as individualistic and local as the actions designed to perpetuate it. Local players, public and private, bankers and entrepreneurs, have an essential role to play in this. States can guide them and, above all, must coordinate their actions so that the whole world moves as one in the same direction. An ecological or health crisis in one country must not be allowed to topple the beautiful house of cards erected through the pursuit of exceedingly independent policies.

The concert of nations is therefore the necessary counterpart, at the other extreme of the spectrum, to grassroots actions. In this concert of nations, we must guard against misplaced nationalism. At the end of the day, we are talking about human lives, and each one is worth as much as the next. It would be an illusion to imagine the world might adopt a democratic system of governance, but it seems legitimate that this concert of nations should give each state a place in proportion to its "burden of souls". China should therefore regain the leadership of the world economy that it claims as its own and which it held for eighteen of the last twenty centuries, before being overtaken by the European continent in the 19th century and then the United States in the 20th century. India, though far removed from our way of life and way of thinking, must be listened to much more than the United States. And Europe will only have a real say if it appears as a real construct and not simply a debating chamber for countries too proud to stand as one on vital issues.

Such a concert of nations, which supposes there be wise leaders or at least leaders imbued with a collective awareness of our common challenges, cannot be harmonious if it can be interrupted at any time by the firecrackers of uncultured hordes. A common concern, more directly tangible than global warming, unites families and governments the world over: terrorism. A recurrent occurrence in human history, recourse to indiscriminate violence is intended or calculated to provoke a state of terror, forcing the opponent into submission before dominating him. The opponent is the population, which is reason enough to condemn such actions. Justifications, excuses and defences will be put forward to explain inhumane behaviours, terrorists invoking ideological principles, usually religious or political, which are misunderstood and perverted at every opportunity. It is a little-known fact that banks in most countries play an important role in uncovering the activities of terrorist groups because terrorism financing involves raising, moving and using funds. In the world of tomorrow, a more responsible world, one can imagine that cooperation between states will go even further than it does today to eradicate terrorist obscurantism as it would a deadly virus.

Pessimists will have no trouble dismissing as illusory the ways forward emerging before our eyes in this crisis. The appeal to the wisdom of the world leaders is not guaranteed to meet with an immediate favourable response and, even less so, to be rapidly followed by action. Simplifying banking regulations, which is supposed to free up the banks' energy and resources, could end up enriching bankers if it leads to excessive speculation.

There have been setbacks before, from the unfulfilled hopes there would be a peaceful future when the League of Nations was set up to the financial disaster that followed the dismantling of the Glass–Steagall Act. But, that's forgetting that the world has changed: political and corporate leaders alike are under constant and very public scrutiny, with social networks just a click away to denounce any departures from what is acceptable. Today's world, with a freedom of expression, sometimes misused, and an ease of communication, sometimes regrettable, is nonetheless a world where transparency has made immense strides. With transparency necessarily comes accountability. It is an element that needs to be taken into account when imagining how tomorrow's world will function, an element of *de facto* if not de jure governance, a kind of democracy 2.0 for the most enthusiastic, or a real warning system for the more cautious.

The adoption of hybrid working (everywhere and particularly in financial institutions), banks that are once again sufficiently solid to inspire confidence (whose longer-term objectives are to deliver sustainable growth in their territories and for their customers to have a healthier, more serene life), governments coordinating efforts (focused on improving the health of the population and planet), the removal of counterproductive regulations hampering the banking sector, increased transparency leading to greater accountability on the part of everyone — those are the ways ahead out of the crisis. This can be a path to happy, healthy and sustainable growth. It is up to us, bankers and economists, to explain it, finance it, in short make it possible.

Bibliography

Allen, L. and Bali, T. (2004), Cyclicality in Catastrophic and Operational Risk Measurements, Working Paper, Baruch College, Cuny.

Allen, L., Boudoukh, J. and Saunders, A. (2004), *Understanding Market, Credit, and Operational Risk: The Value at Risk Approach*. Blackwell Publishing, Malden, MA; Oxford, UK; Carlton, Victoria, Australia.

Amin, G. and Kat, H. (2001), Welcome to the Dark Side: Hedge Fund Attribution and Survivorship Bias over the Period 1994–2001, *Journal of Alternative Investments*, vol. 6, issue 1, pp. 57–73.

Anson, J. P., Fabozzi, F. J., Choudhry, M. and Chen, R. R. (2004). *Credit Derivatives: Instruments, Applications and Pricing*, John Wiley & Sons, Inc. Hoboken, NJ.

Berger, A. N., Herring, R. J. and Szegö, G. P. (June 1995), The Role of Capital in Financial Institutions, *Journal of Banking and Finance*, vol. 19, issue 3–4, pp. 393–430.

Bernanke, B. S. (1993), Credit in the Macroeconomy, *Federal Reserve Bank of New York, Quarterly Review*, Spring 1992–93.

Bernanke, B. and Gertler, M. (1995), Inside the Black Box: The Credit Channel of Monetary Policy Transmission, *Journal of Economic Perspectives*, vol. 9, issue 4, pp. 27–48.

Bernanke, B. S. and Blinder, A. (1988), Credit, Money and Aggregate Demand, *The American Economic Review*, vol. 78, issue 2, pp. 435–439, published by the American Economic Association.

Bernanke, B. S. and Gertler, M. (March 1989), Agency Costs, Net Worth, and Business Fluctuations, *The American Economic Review*, vol. 79, issue 1, pp. 14–31.

Bernanke, B. S. and James, H. (1991), The Gold Standard, Deflation and Financial Crisis in the Great Depression: An International Comparison, from

Financial Markets and Financial Crises, R. B. Hubbard (Ed.), University of Chicago Press, pp. 33–68.

Bernanke, B. S., Gertler, M. and Gilchrist, S. (1996), The Financial Accelerator and the Flight to Quality, *The Review of Economics and Statistics*, vol. 78, issue 1, pp. 1–15.

Bernanke, B. S., Gertler, M. and Gilchrist, S. (1999), The Financial Accelerator in a Quantitative Business Cycle Framework, from *Handbook of Macroeconomics*, J. B. Taylor and M. Woodford (Eds.), Elsevier North-Holland, Amsterdam, chap. 21, pp. 1341–1393.

Blinder, A. S. and Stiglitz, J. E. (1983), Money, Credit Constraints, and Economic Activity, *The American Economic Review*, vol. 73, issue 2, pp. 297–302.

Blundell-Wignall A. (2007), Structured Products: Implications for Financial Market, *Financial Market Trends*, OECD.

Buiter, W. (2007), Lesson from the 2007 Financial Crisis, *CEPR Policy Insight*, issue 18, pp. 1–17.

Campbell, A. (2008). VaR Counts, Risk.net, available at https://www.risk.net/risk-management/market-risk/1498476/var-counts

Carlstrom, C. T. and Fuerst, T. S. (1997), Agency Costs, Net Worth, and Business Fluctuations: A Computable General Equilibrium Analysis, *The American Economic Review*, vol. 87, issue 5, pp. 893–910.

Castel, M. and Plihon, D. (2008), recommend the article Rudes leçons de la crise financière, Le Monde, 1 February 2008.

Cherubini, U., Luciano, E. and Vecchiato, W. (2004), *Copula Methods in Finance*, John Wiley & Sons Ltd, Chichester, England.

Cossin, P. and Pirotte, H. (2000), *Advanced Credit Risk Analysis: Financial Approaches and Mathematical Models to Assess, Price, and Manage Credit Risk*, Wiley Series in Financial Engineering, John Wiley & Sons, Inc.

Crouhy, M., Galai, D. and Mark, R. (2006), *The Essentials of Risk Management*, Kindle Edition, McGraw Hill, New York.

Cummins, J. D., Lewis, C. M. and We, R. (2004), The Market Value Impact of Operational Risk Events for U.S. Banks and Insurers, *Journal of Banking & Finance*, vol. 30, issue 10, pp. 2605–2634.

Danielsson, J., Taylor, A. and Zigrand, J. P. (2005), Highwaymen or Heroes: Should Hedge Funds Be Regulated?, *Journal of Financial Stability*, vol. 1, issue 4, pp. 522–543.

Dell'ariccia, G., Igan, D. and Laeven, L. (2008), Credit Booms and Lending Standards: Evidence from the Subprime Mortgage Market, IMF Working Paper 08/106.

Diamond, D. W. and Dybvig, P. H. (1983). Bank Runs, Deposit Insurance, and Liquidity, *Journal of Political Economy*, vol. 91, issue 3, pp. 401–418.

Fisher, I. (1933), The Debt-Deflation Theory of Great Depressions, *Econometrica*, vol. 1, issue 4, pp. 337–357.

Friedman, M. and Schwartz Jacobson, A. (1963), *A Monetary History of the United States, 1867–1960*, Princeton University Press, Princeton, NJ.

Fuerst, T. S. (1992), Liquidity, Loanable Funds, and Real Activity, *Journal of Monetary Economics*, vol. 29, issue 1, pp. 3–24.

Garbaravicius, T. and Dierick, F. (2005), Hedge Funds and Their Implication for Financial Stability, ECB Occasional Paper Series, no. 34, available from https://www.ecb.europa.eu/pub/pdf/other/ecbocp34en.pdf

Gertler, M. (1988), Financial Structure and Aggregate Activity: An Overview, *Journal of Money, Credit, and Banking*, vol. 20, issue 3, part 2, pp. 559–588, published by Ohio State University Press.

Gertler, M. and Gilchrist, S. (1993), The Role of Credit Market Imperfections in The Monetary Transmission Mechanism: Arguments and Evidence, *The Scandinavian Journal of Economics*, vol. 95, issue 1, pp. 43–64.

Gertler, M. and Gilchrist, S. (1994), Monetary Policy, Business Cycles and the Behavior of Small Manufacturing Firms, *The Quarterly Journal of Economics*, vol. 109, issue 2, pp. 309–340.

Goodhart, C. (2008), Liquidity Risk Management, *Financial Stability Review*, Banque de France, Special Issue 11, pp. 39–44.

Gorton, G. and Pennacchi, G. (1990), Financial Intermediaries and Liquidity Creation, *Journal of Finance*, vol. 45, issue 1, pp. 49–71.

Hildebrand, P. (2007), The Challenge of Sovereign Wealth Funds, speech at the International Center for Monetary and Banking Studies in Geneva, available at https://www.snb.ch/fr/publications/communication/speeches/2007/ref_20071218_pmh

Honda, Y., Kawahara, F., Kohara, H. (1995), Credit Crunch in Japan, Discussion Paper, no. 8, Research Institute, Ministry of Post and Communication.

Hubbard, R. G. (1995), Is There a Credit Channel for Monetary Policy?, *Federal Reserve Bank of St Louis Review*, issue May, pp. 63–77.

Jackson, P., Maude, D. and Perraudin, W. (1997), Bank Capital and Value at Risk, Bank of England, available at https://www.bankofengland.co.uk/-/media/boe/files/working-paper/1998/bank-capital-and-value-at-risk.pdf

Jaffee, D. and Russel, T. (1976), Imperfect Information, Uncertainty, and Credit Rationing, *The Quarterly Journal of Economics*, vol. 90, issue 4, pp. 651–666.

Jaffee, D. and Stiglitz, J. E. (1990). Credit Rationing, from *The Handbook of Monetary Economics*, B. Friedman and F. Hahn (Eds.), vol. 2, Elsevier, Amsterdam, pp. 837–888.

Karpoff, J. and Lott, J. R. (1993), The Reputational Penalty Firm Bear for Committing Criminal Fraud, *The Journal of Law and Economics*, vol. 36, issue 2, pp. 757–802.

Kashyap, A. K. and Stein, J. C. (1994), Monetary Policy and Bank Lending, from *Monetary Policy*, N. G. Mankiw (Ed.), National Bureau of Economic Research, pp. 221–261.

Kashyap, A. K., Lamont, O. A. and Stein, J. C. (1994), Credit Conditions and Cyclical Behavior of Inventories, *The Quarterly Journal of Economics*, vol. 109, issue 3, pp. 565–592.

Kashyap, A. K., Stein, J. C. and Wilcox, D. W. (1993), Monetary Policy and Credit Conditions: Evidence from the Composition of External Finance, *American Economic Review*, vol. 83, issue 1, pp. 78–98.

King, S. R. (1986), Monetary Transmission: Through Bank Loans or Bank Liabilities?, *Journal of Money, Credit, and Banking*, vol. 18, issue 3, pp. 290–303.

Kiyotaki, N. and Moore, J. (1997), Credit Cycles, *Journal of Political Economy*, vol. 105, issue 2, pp. 211–248, published by University of Chicago Press.

Malkiel, B. and Saha, A. (2005), Hedge Funds: Risk and Return, *Financial Analysts Journal*, vol. 61, issue 6, pp. 80–88, published by Taylor & Francis, Ltd.

Mc Carthy Callum (2007), Transparency Requirements and Hedge Funds, *Financial Stability Review*, Banque de France, Special Issue Hedge Funds, pp. 77–84.

Mishkin, F. S. (1978), The Household Balance Sheet and the Great Depression, *The Journal of Economic History*, vol. 38, issue 4, pp. 918–937.

Mishkin, F. S. (1994), Preventing Financial Crises: An International Perspective, *The Manchester School of Economic & Social Studies*, vol. 62, issue 0, pp. 1–40.

Mishkin, F. S. (2004), *Monnaie, banque et marchés financiers,* 7th Edition, Pearson Education France, Paris.

Oliner, S. D. and Rudebusch, G. D. (1996), Is There a Broad Credit Channel for Monetary Policy?, *Federal Reserve Bank of San Francisco, Economic Review*, vol. 1, pp. 3–13.

Owens, R. E. and Schreft, S. L. (1993), Identifying Credit Crunches, Research Department, Federal Reserve Bank of Richmond, Working Paper 93-02.

Palmrose, Z., Richardson, V. J. and Scholtz, S. (2004), Determinants of Market Reactions to Restatement Announcement, *Journal of Accounting and Economics*, vol. 37, issue 1, pp. 59–89.

Peicuti, C. (2010), *Crédit, déstabilisation et crises*, Edition L'Harmattan, Paris.

Peicuti, C. (2013), Securitization and the Subprime Mortgage Crisis, *Journal of Post Keynesian Economics*, vol. 35, issue 3, pp. 443–456.

Peicuti, C. (2014), The Great Depression and the Great Recession: A Comparative Analysis of Their Analogies, *The European Journal of Comparative Economics*, vol. 11, issue 1, pp. 55–78.

Perry, J. and Fontnouvelle, P. (2005), Measuring Reputational Risk: The Market Reaction to Operational Loss Announcements, Federal Reserve Bank of Boston, available at SSRN: https://ssrn.com/abstract=861364 or http://dx.doi.org/10.2139/ssrn.861364

Rachev, S. T., Chernobai, A. S. and Fabozzi, F. J. (2007), *Operational Risk, a Guide to Basel II Capital Requirements, Models, and Analysis*, Wiley, Hoboken, NJ.

Rajan, R. (1992), Insiders and Outsiders: The Choice between Relationship and Arm's Length Debt, *The Journal of Finance*, vol. 47, issue 4, pp. 1367–1400.

Ramey, V. (1993), How Important Is the Credit Channel in the Transmission of Monetary Policy?, *Carnegie-Rochester Conference Series on Public Policy*, vol. 39, pp. 1–45.

Romer, C. D. and Romer, D. H. (1990), New Evidence on the Monetary Transmission Mechanism, *Brookings Papers on Economic Activity*, vol. 1, pp. 149–213.

Schmidt, R. H. (2001), Differences between Financial Systems in European Countries: Consequences for EMU, from *The Monetary Transmission Process: Recent Developments and Lessons for Europe*, Deutsche Bundesbank (Ed.), Palgrave Macmillan, London.

Sharpe, S. (1990), Asymmetric Information, Bank Lending and Implicit Contracts: A Stylized Model of Customer Relationships, *Journal of Finance*, vol. 45, issue 4, pp. 1069–1087.

Stiglitz, J. E. and Weiss, A. (1981), Credit Rationing in Markets with Imperfect Information, *The American Economic Review*, vol. 71, issue 3, pp. 393–410, published by the American Economic Association.

Taylor, J. (1995), The Monetary Transmission Mechanism: An Empirical Framework, *The Journal of Economic Perspectives*, vol. 9, issue 4, pp. 11–26.

Tobin, J. (1969). A General Equilibrium Approach to Monetary Theory, *Journal of Money Credit and Banking*, vol. 1, issue 1, pp. 15–29, published by Ohio State University Press.

Williamson, S. D. (1986). Costly Monitoring, Financial Intermediation and Equilibrium Credit Rationing, *Journal of Monetary Economics*, vol. 18, issue 2, pp. 159–179.

Williamson, S. D. (1987a), Costly Monitoring, Loan Contracts, and Equilibrium Credit Rationing, *The Quarterly Journal of Economics*, vol. 102, issue 1, pp. 135–145.

Williamson, S. D. (1987b), Financial Intermediation, Business Failures, and Real Business Cycles, *Journal of Political Economy*, vol. 95, issue 6, pp. 1196–1216.

Wilson, T. (1997a), Portfolio Credit Risk I, from *Credit Risk Models and Management*, Risk Books, London, pp. 55–74.

Wilson, T. (1997b), Portfolio Credit Risk II, from *Risk: Managing Risk in the World's Financial Markets*, Incisive Financial Publ, London, vol. 10, issue 10, pp. 56–62.

Name Index

A

Albert, Calmette, 63
Apollinaire, Guillaume, 59

B

Barbier, Marguerite, 59
Biden, Joe, 13, 48, 65, 103–108
Blinken, Antony, 108
Bolsonaro, Jair, 5, 8
Broderick, Joseph, 10
Buffett, Warren, 51
Bush, George W., 45–46

C

Calignon, Guillaume de, 23
Calmette, Albert, 63
Céline, Louis-Ferdinand, 3
Chan, Margaret, 96
Chirac, Jacques, 47
Clinton, Bill, 13
Clinton, Hillary, 52
Colbert, Jean-Baptiste, 35–36

D

da Vinci, Leonardo, 97
Deng Xiaoping, 103, 106

E

Erzberger, Matthias, 41

F

Flahault, Antoine, 19
Fromkin, David, 40

G

Garret, Ron, 51
Getty, Jean Paul, 33
Gide, Charles, vii
Giscard d'Estaing, Valéry, 43
Goldschmidt, Robert, 51
Goubert, Pierre, 35–36
Guérin, Camille, 63
Guillaume, Pierre, 59

H

Harrison, George, 10
Himmler, Heinrich, 41
Hitler, Adolf, 3, 41
Houellebecq, Michel, 57, 133
Hultin, Johan, 58

J

Johnson, Boris, 8

K

Kalathil, Shanthi, 107

L

Le Pen, Marine, 47
Louis XIV, 34–35
Louis XV, 36
Louis XVI, 36–37
Louis XVIII, 40
Ludendorff, Erich, 41

M

Macron, Emmanuel, 22, 28, 47
Mao Zedong, 106
Mazarin, Jules, 35
Mélenchon, Jean-Luc, 47
Mirabeau, 38
Mlambo-Ngcuka, Phumzile, 6

N

Napoleon, 38–39
Napoleon III, 39
Necker, Jacques, 37
Nouy, Danièle, 85

P

Pasteur, Louis, 20–21
Philippe IV, 34

R

Ramos, Gabriela, 6
Rey, Alain, 33
Reynolds, Jackson, 10
Rohrer, Mario, 98
Roosevelt, Teddy, 13
Rostand, Edmond, 59

S

Salvini, Matthew, 8
Sarkozy Nicolas, 43–47
Stiglitz, Joseph, 12, 50–51

T

Talleyrand-Périgord, Charles-Maurice
    de, 40–41, 61
Terray, Abbot Joseph Marie, 36
Trump, Donald, 4, 8, 13, 47–48,
    51–52, 55, 103, 105–107, 115
Turgot, Robert Jacques, 37

W

Wang Yi, 108

X

Xi Jinping, 106

Y

Yang Jiechi, 108

www.ingramcontent.com/pod-product-compliance
Lightning Source LLC
Chambersburg PA
CBHW061253220326
41599CB00028B/5638